THE CHRISTOPHER REEVE SCRAPBOOK

BY MARGERY STEINBERG

tempo
books
GROSSET & DUNLAP
A Filmways Company
Publishers • New York

The Christopher Reeve Scrapbook
Copyright © 1981 by Margery Steinberg
ISBN: 0-448-17223-2
Cover photo by Donald Sanders/Globe Photos
All rights reserved
A Tempo Books Original
Tempo Books is registered in the United States Patent Office
Published simultaneously in Canada
Printed in the United States of America
First Ace Tempo Printing: June 1981

DEDICATION
With thanks to Lew for his invaluable assistance
and his never-ending energy.

Table of Contents

I
Introduction

"Part of being an actor is taking risks . . ."

People say he came out of nowhere. From unknown actor to world-famous superstar rose Christopher Reeve. The role of Superman helped him fulfill a dream.

"When I was a kid in Princeton," Chris recalls, "we used to see George Reeves in those television cheapies as 'Superman.' The others would ask me if I was kin to George Reeves, and I wouldn't deny that I was even though my name is a singular Reeve." Chris always believed he would be famous some day, but he didn't know how or why.

Handsome as a movie star and just big enough at 6 feet 4 inches, 190 pounds, Chris had just the right combination to secure the part of the "Man of Steel." Education and preparation for an acting career have helped to bring about his present success. He has the right attitude, too.

"Part of being an actor is taking risks—saying, 'I

dare to do this!' If you're going to be an actor, part of the definition of the work is someone who'll accept and try for challenging roles," says Chris.

It took a lot of courage for him to try out for such a demanding role. Yet his acting of the two separate personalities of Clark Kent and Superman was so convincing that he won the part.

"Superman may be able to leap tall buildings, but can he make the leap from the '50s to the '70s?" wondered the actor. Chris's concern was whether audiences would believe his modern-day portrayal of the legendary superhero. He knew that if *Superman* didn't fly as forecast, the name Christopher Reeve might never be heard again.

Chris doesn't have to worry about his future, though. Although reviewers weren't overly complimentary to the movie as a whole, most of them raved about Chris's performance as Superman/Clark Kent. Since the movie had such a high budget and ran a huge publicity campaign, well-known and even obscure publications reviewed the film.

Critic Pauline Kael wrote in the *New Yorker*: "Christopher Reeve, the young actor chosen to play the lead in *Superman*, is the best reason to see the movie. He has an open-faced, deadpan style that's just right for a windup hero. Reeve plays innocent but not dumb, and the combination of his Pop jawline and physique with his unassuming manner makes him immediately likable. In this role, Reeve comes close to being a living equivalent of comic-strip art . . . But *Superman*, one of the two or three most expensive movies ever made, and with the biggest event promotion yet, is a cheesy-looking film . . ."

Ms. Kael expressed concern about the plot not fitting together well, and about the unconvincing performances of some of the other actors. But she returned to her praise of Chris's performance saying, "The film rallies when Reeve takes over—especially when he gets out of the drably staged scenes at the offices of the *Daily Planet,* gets into his red cape and blue tights, files over Metropolis, and performs a string of miracles."

Michael Korda, a reviewer for *Glamor* magazine, said he found *Superman* more interesting than a lot of movies he had seen recently, but begins by pointing out the movie's problems. "*Superman* suffers from the defects of its own size and expense, rather like those circus giants who can't stand up without help because they're so big, their muscles aren't strong enough to carry them." He says that Chris put much more than one would expect any actor to put into such a role, and "succeeds in awakening both our sympathy for Superman's difficult double role and our belief that he really *is* both people—no mean feat!"

Ken Fulton for *Boys' Life* wrote about the special effects and heroic deals that made *Superman* a success. Complimenting the star he said, "Portraying the native of Krypton is a brilliant young actor, skier, sailor and pilot Christopher Reeve."

A writer for *America* magazine said that the two central figures, Chris and Margot Kidder, seemed to be enjoying themselves, and thus the audience became enthusiastic about the movie. "Most of the credit must go to the engaging performances of the two principals, Christopher Reeve in the title role and Margot Kidder as Lois."

Movie and TV critic Judith Crist wrote, "Thanks to an excellent Broadway actor, Christopher Reeve, Clark Kent and Superman come to brilliant one-dimensional life . . ."

An article in *Newsweek* magazine said that *Superman* made Christopher Reeve the fastest-rising star in recent years. Commenting on his acting the reviewer said, "Christopher Reeve's entire performance is a delight. Ridiculously good-looking, with a face as sharp and strong as an ax blade, his bumbling, fumbling Clark Kent and omnipotent Superman are simply two types of gallantry and innocence."

One writer even affectionately called Chris "a mammoth box of Wheaties."

The actor anxiously studied every column and review to find out what people thought of his performance. He had worked so hard to get to the point of being a star—it didn't just happen overnight. Putting forth a serious effort, taking advantage of the right opportunities, applying what he learned from his experiences, and having the gift of good looks, all contributed to the transformation of this mild-mannered young actor into an unbelievable superstar. Just how did he do it?

II
The Early Years

"Actually, I've been very lucky and I know it."

Born in New York on September 25, 1952, Chris was a member of a non-show business family. His actor qualities began to develop in the early years of his childhood. He and his younger brother would climb inside cardboard grocery cartons and pretend they were sailing on pirate ships. "To us they became ships, simply because we said they were," Chris recalls. Some of this childhood innocence and imagination has also helped him become a great actor.

Chris says that his growing-up years were rather quiet until his involvement in the theater. He lived in Princeton, New Jersey, a university town. And Princetown University has had a great influence on the activities of the town. There are a variety of cultural events and a number of small schools, but very little business activity. Its many historical points of interest as well as its quiet academic atmosphere have attracted many students to Princeton. Growing up there was very different from growing up in the big city, but it offered just the right combination for Christopher Reeve.

His real acting career began at the early age of nine. When most children are just beginning to learn the three R's in school, he was taking on the added responsibility of rehearsals and performances. His first opportunity occurred quite by accident.

Because of his parents' high interest in education, Chris attended the prestigious Princeton Day private elementary school. One day someone from the local McCarter Theater came to his school looking for a boy soprano. Chris's class at the time was studying dinosaurs and other stuff which didn't interest him at all. So he volunteered to audition. And, much to his surprise, he got the part. The play was Gilbert and Sullivan's Operetta *Yeoman of the Guard.*

Two days later he was attending rehearsals on a regular basis. He didn't seem to mind missing school either. "It was really quite something," he laughs. "Everybody else in school was sitting there working on some test in third period, but I'd look at my watch and when it was 10:15, I'd excuse myself and go to the matinee at the theater."

Being an actor made him feel special. He felt good about being able to do something that the other kids couldn't do. "Being somebody else took me away from a lot of things I was not prepared to deal with," Chris recalls.

The McCarter Theater gave Chris the opportunity to gain his initial acting experience. The company began in 1960 and was closely tied to Princeton University. In addition to some six plays performed by members of the group, the organization was also responsible for bringing other talents and acts to the local area. Classical and popular music, dance and films were all part of their program. Many famous actors and actresses have acted with the group at some point in their careers.

Recently, such well-known actors as Peggy Cass, Dina Merrill and Herschel Bernardi have performed with the McCarter Theater.

Chris's interest in the theater continued when at age fifteen he was hired as an apprentice at the Williamstown Playhouse in Williamstown, Massachusetts, for summer stock productions. This group was dedicated to the development of new writing, acting and musical talent. There he learned much about the workings of a theater, assisted the actors and directors, and tried some acting.

At sixteen he got his Actors' Equity Card and he was on his way to stardom.

Actors' Equity Association, usually called Equity, is a trade union for actors. It was started in 1913 to protect actors from unfair treatment by producers. An open union, anybody who is offered a job in the theater may join. Chris took advantage of the opportunity. He joined and paid the initiation fee and moderate yearly dues. People who want to be actors must join, since only Equity members may appear in professional productions.

Some of the ways in which the Equity contract protects the actors are: minimum salaries, rehearsal pay, limitations on rehearsal times, regulations on costumes, transportation and publicity.

Chris's early acting career includes a long list of a variety of different experiences. He played roles in such widely respected theaters as the Boothbay (Maine) Playhouse, the San Diego (California) Shakespeare Festival and the Loeb Drama Center (Massachusetts). His parts included that of Victor in *Private Lives*, Aeneas in *Troilus and Cressida* (Shakespeare), Beliaev in *A Month in the Country*, Macbeth in *Threepenny Opera*, and Kid in *Our Town*. Other plays to his credit are *The Games*, *Death of a Salesman*, *The Hostage*, and another Shakespearean work, *Much Ado About Nothing*.

Chris has played so many different kinds of roles —some comedy, some dramas—which have given him a variety of acting skills that will be invaluable throughout his career. This kind of experience also helps actors audition and get many parts without being stereotyped into one specific role, such as always playing the villain, or always the father.

For his college years, Chris selected Cornell University, a fairly large school in Ithaca, New York. A prestigious Ivy League school, Cornell's largest unit is the College of Arts and Sciences, where Chris enrolled. Again choosing a field of study related to his interest in the theater, he majored in English and Music Theory.

While in college Chris hired an acting agent and launched his career. He hustled parts in New York.

Quite often he would cut classes, go to New York, audition for film and television parts, and then travel several hours back to Cornell in the same day. Then, of course, he would have to make up all of the work he missed. But Chris says it was all worth the trouble. While at college he did get occasional TV spots. He also took a European sabbatical to check out the Old Vic and the Comedie Française. These were well-known repertory theater companies.

Old Vic is a London, England, theater which dates back to 1818. It specializes in drama, mostly Shakespearean, and opera. Chris was hired for backstage work, where he served as a glorified errand boy for a while. Then he worked as a dialect coach for British actors in American plays. He helped players in such productions as *The Front Page* pronounce words correctly according to the American way of speaking.

Comedie Française is the oldest French state theater founded in the seventeenth century. It is famous for its classical and modern repertory productions. Chris's stay there was relatively short, but he did have the opportunity to observe the different theater techniques used by the company.

Chris then took advantage of a skiing holiday in Switzerland. It gave him a chance to relax and unwind before returning to the United States.

During his senior year back at Cornell, Chris was one of three people admitted to the advanced program at the Juilliard School for Drama in New York City. This world-famous school for musicians and actors has a professional actor training program. It offers aspiring stars the opportunity to study all means of dramatic expression. Importance is placed on the growth of the actor's physical, technical and cultural skills. Students are encouraged to develop attitudes which will help them to be creative, experimental and expressive in each and every acting role they try.

At Juilliard, Chris worked among many famous people. Robin Williams ("Mork and Mindy") was a classmate, and the well-known John Houseman ("Paper Chase") was his master teacher. Some of the valuable training Chris received included voice work, ballet, fencing, stage fighting, acrobatics, circus and mime. All of these skills have helped him to be successful in his variety of acting roles.

He led an extremely busy life juggling his senior year in college and the first year of study at Juilliard at the same time. So, as before, he had to travel back and forth between the two schools. At the end of that difficult year, Chris received his BA in Literature from Cornell. But he still had another year to study at Juilliard.

Chris's next big accomplishment as an actor— and big it turned out to be—was to win the role of Ben Harper in the long-running daily television serial "Love of Life." At first the show's producers had intended their new character to appear only once or twice a week. But Chris became so popular with the viewers that he was on four or five times a week.

What was so ironic about the situation was that

Chris had only taken the job to pay for his second year of training at Juilliard. When he began to be on a daily basis on "Love of Life," he didn't have time to attend classes. He had to quit Juilliard and ended up being on TV for two years.

Ben Harper was such a detestable character. Little old ladies were known to attack Chris Reeve when they saw him in public places, forgetting that he wasn't really Ben.

The television series, also known as a "soap opera" began on September 24, 1951—a year before Chris was even born. It was created by Roy Winsor and directed by Larry Auerbach—to whom the show owes its success. The continuing story had the small imaginary town of Rosehill as its locale. It was centered around Bruce and Vanessa Sterling, and the problems of their family and friends. Vanessa has a willful sister named Meg who tried to control the lives of everyone with whom she had any contact. Vanessa, who loved life (thus the title "Love of Life"), married but was soon widowed. Meg married and had a baby. But by 1958 (seven years after the show began) Meg was divorcing her husband. Many different "sensational" conflicts took place in the story.

Chris Reeve did not play the role of Ben Harper for the entire run of the show. But the character was Meg's son, a very devious, lawbreaking, and immoral individual. This was very much out of character with Chris's real personality, but all of his training enabled him to play the role very well.

During the first week in February 1980, after a

twenty-eight-year run, "Love of Life" went off the air. It was TV's oldest serial (beginning the same year as "Search for Tomorrow"). CBS cancelled the show when a new 4 P.M. time slot caused the show to lose much of its audience.

Many well-known performers appeared in "Love of Life" during its run. Peter Falk ("Columbo") Roy Scheider (Jaws), Bert Convy ("Tattletales"), and Ja'net DuBois ("Good Times") had parts. The show also helped launch the acting careers of such stars as Warren Beatty, Marsha Mason, Anne Jackson, Ellen Burstyn, Lee Grant, Sandy Dennis and of course, Christopher Reeve. Sammy Davis Jr. was such a fan of the show that he made a guest appearance on it. One famous actor said of his soap opera days, "It's good training; you learn to improvise because you don't know what's going to happen next."

Larry Auerbach was the show's director since the beginning of the series. His techniques have proven very helpful to budding new actors. He let the actor plan the next move in the scene for himself—in a sense almost ad lib the next action. Each scene was rehearsed maybe three or four times, after which the actor really began to remember the lines. The atmosphere of the rehearsal room was not so serious in contrast to the seriousness of the scripts. Taping schedules were so tight that the actors were together for long periods of time. The feeling of "family" developed among the people and they helped each other as a team.

Originally the program was performed live in a

studio on East 85th Street in New York. But with the beginning of color TV and the ability to tape shows in advance, CBS (this show's network) moved its operations to a new production center on West 57th Street.

The taping of shows made things a little less hectic than they were in the days of live broadcast. But even with modern facilities, a complete show had to be rehearsed, blocked and taped within 12 hours. Actors accidentally called each other by their real names on-camera. Sometimes they got confused by stage setups and walked through fake walls. Chris has fond memories of his television days.

Soap operas were started back in 1933 by the famous soap manufacturer Procter and Gamble. They designed a creative radio advertisement to sell their soap. Oxydol's "Own Ma Perkins" was aired in Chicago. The commercial message was skillfully hidden in a dramatic story. "Soaps" caught on and were sponsored by other manufacturers. A writer named Irna Phillips is credited with associating the soap opera to family life.

The average soap opera program has 6.7 million viewers according to the A.C. Nielsen rating. These shows appeal to many different types of people. The stories are related to what's happening in today's society. The characters and events reflect the changing values and interests of many American people.

Soap operas have become the most powerful entertainment on or off television. No play or movie receives such long-term devotion of its fans. No other television show regularly attracts such large numbers of viewers. Soap operas provide the opportunity for a beginning actor to perform in front of extremely large audiences, and to become known by so many people. What a way to begin a career!

Getting the part in "Love of Life" was important to Christopher Reeve and to his career. First of all, the two years he was in the soap opera enabled him to pay back the money his stepfather loaned him for his education. Also, the experience of television acting was very different from any he previously had in the theater.

During those busy years, Chris also tried to get parts in plays as often as possible. He worked with two well-known New York Companies—The Circle Repertory Company and The Manhattan Theater Club.

The Circle Repertory is a top-notch off-Broadway group. It was started in 1969 by a group of actors who joined together to share their artistic goals. The company devotes itself to the production of works of the finest new American writers, and tries to help the audience experience the action of the play.

The Manhattan Theater Club began in 1970 as a multi-theater, non-profit organization. Its purpose is to present new works as well as some opera, classical plays, poetry series, music and classroom experiences. Performances take place in a number of small theaters around New York City.

With all of these wonderful opportunities, there was no doubt that his career was going to start soaring! "Actually, I've been very lucky and I know it," says Chris.

III
Broadway Debut

"She (Katharine Hepburn) was a wonderful lady
. . . But I was too nervous to do well."

Chris led a very busy life during those two years
in the soap opera. Between show tapings and audi-
tioning for acting jobs, he landed a part in a new
Broadway play in 1976. Famous actress Katharine
Hepburn was chosen for the leading role of Mrs.
Basil. Chris, of course, was thrilled to have the opportunity to play opposite such a star.

The play, *A Matter of Gravity*, was written by the
well-known English author Enid Bagnold (who
also wrote the books *National Velvet*, *Serene Blan-
dish*, and another play, *The Chalk Garden*).

Chris played Mrs. Basil's grandson, Nicky. The
setting was a once beautiful mansion which had become run-down. In the play, Mrs. Basil was an
elderly, but very wealthy woman. She had very traditional social values, and was not sure what to
think about the young around her. Because she was

so old, however, she gave her estate to her grandson and took up residence in a home for old people. Grandson Nicky, although graduated from the very fine traditional school, Oxford, had rather modern ideas about life. The conflict between the characters created the story. The play was described as being "a comedy about life and death." *Newsweek* magazine called it "a comedy of bad manners."

Before opening on Broadway, the show was tested in a number of cities around the country. For several weeks the actors traveled from place to place. At one point during its run in San Diego, California, the star had to perform in a wheelchair. Ms. Hepburn had broken her ankle. As they say in show business "The show must go on!" Luckily, the actress soon recovered.

The show had a relatively short run on Broadway, and was considered by some people as being "not very good." But nonetheless it was good experience for an aspiring actor.

Actually, Chris received some good reviews for his performance. "Christopher Reeve is making his Broadway debut as Miss Hepburn's stage grandson," wrote Broadway theater critic Emory Lewis. "He succeeds admirably in the difficult role . . ."

Chris really enjoyed acting with Katharine Hepburn and says she taught him a lot. He remembers, "She used to say to me, 'Now be fascinating, Christopher, now be fascinating.' " I would say, 'Well, that's easy for you to say. The rest of us have to work at it, you know.' "

And he did work extremely hard. Even though people liked his acting in the play, Chris felt he could have done better. "She (Katharine Hepburn) was a wonderful lady," he insists, "But I was too nervous to do well."

It was a very difficult time for Chris because he led such a busy life. In order to meet the schedules for both the New York soap opera and the pre-Broadway road tour, he had to spend a lot of time traveling. Some days he had to be out by 4:00 A.M. to catch a plane to New York. On the way he would learn the lines for the day's taping of "Love of Life." He had to arrive at CBS studios by 7:30 A.M. and work all day until 5:00 P.M. Then he would hop another plane at 6:00 and shuttle back to Washington, Philadelphia, New Haven, Boston, Toronto, or wherever that nights' performance of *A Matter of Gravity* was. That schedule went on for some sixteen weeks, until the play opened in New York.

Chris was very thin then. He was only 188 pounds which is a very low weight for a person of his height. He was sometimes called "the toothpick kid." "I was really in poor shape back then," Chris admits.

The next year Chris had still another opportunity to further his career. He was selected for a small role in a movie entitled *Gray Lady Down*. Universal Pictures was filming the picture for March 1978 release. The producer was Walter Mirisch and the director David Greene, both well-known in Hollywood. The story was based on the novel *Event 1000*

by David Lavallee, and the screenplay was written
by James Whittaker and Howard Sackler.

From the title, you might think the movie was
just another picture about horses. But it wasn't.
The film, rated PG, was a kind of disaster movie
about a damaged submarine that was resting on
the bottom of the sea off the coast of Bermuda.
The cast included Charlton Heston, David Carradine, Stacy Keach, Ned Beatty, and Christopher Reeve.

In the story the occupants of the sunken submarine were growing fearful that they might die
due to lack of air or too much water. On the surface expensive efforts were being made to rescue
them. The sophisticated U.S. Navy had invented
something called the DSRV. This machine was
supposed to be able to reach stuck subs, latch onto
the escape hatch and lift the sailors to the water's
surface. In this case, however, the submarine
U.S.S. *Neptune* was lying deep in an ocean trench.
From time to time the rocks and silt below it
shifted and covered up the escape hatch. This made
rescue efforts nearly impossible. The brilliant in-
ventor, played by David Carradine, came up with
the successful idea of using a small two-man sub to
clear the hatch. Then the Navy's DSRV performed
the rescue mission. Ned Beatty acted as David
Carradine's faithful assistant; Stacy Keach was the
officer in charge of the rescue; and Charlton
Heston was the captain on the last voyage of his
career.

A newcomer to films, Christopher Reeve played

only a small role. He went almost unnoticed among this cast of some fine, well-known actors. But, once again, he was thankful for the opportunity to have another career-building experience.

The movie was considered by critics to be "mediocre," and didn't run for very long. It was referred to as "a disaster about a disaster." The one really good thing about the film was its beautiful underwater photography.

Chris's career in movies had only just begun, though. Little did he know then that his next part would make him a star.

IV
Family History

"Being somebody else took me away from a lot of things I was not prepared to deal with."

Christopher Reeve's zodiac sign is Libra. And a true Libran he is. Chris has qualities that balance both sides of the scales. He is romantic, fair and a lover of beauty, while at times he is lazy and tempermental. He loves people but hates large crowds. Librans love the arts, so does Chris. His fantastic Libran ability to concentrate on his work has helped him achieve success as an actor.

According to astrological theory, the Libran must, in all parts of his life, express himself. Chris does this through his acting as well as in his personal friendships with other people. A well-balanced emotional relationship with a member of the opposite sex is also characteristic of his sun sign. Chris does have a steady girl-friend, but he prefers to keep his private life pretty much a secret.

Avoiding quarrels and disagreements with other

people, the Libran tries to be what others want him to be. Chris has natural charm and a good-natured personality. Throughout his acting career he has gotten along with whomever he is working.

The most negative quality of a Libran is indecision. A person of this sign often takes a wait-and-see attitude, and many seem lazy. But when he does decide that he wants something, he generally works hard to get it. Chris also exhibits this characteristic. He says, "I think I've always known I'd be in the limelight. I knew I'd be a success. I simply never had any doubt about it." But he wasn't quite sure how. He had tried many different types of acting, but never really had a big hit.

He now laughs about the time he tried out for a role in a mini-series for TV called "The Captains and The Kings." He was so demoralized when he didn't get the part. Another young actor named Richard Jordan was selected. For some reason, the loss of this role was particularly hard for Chris to handle. He had really built up his hopes of being selected, but it just didn't work out.

He was so down that he stopped working for a few months. Chris wasn't sure which direction he wanted to go in acting. "I sat on the beach at Santa Monica—not even Malibu—for five months. I absolutely wrote myself off," he says. "Then one day I said that isn't right."

Back in New York for only a little while, he found jobs on Broadway and appeared in a bit part in the movie *Gray Lady Down*. But then he received that lucky phone call inviting him to audition for *Superman*. His success had just begun.

The fact that Christopher Reeve had high aspirations is not surprising. He comes from a well-educated and high-achieving family.

His parents were divorced when Chris was four years old. He was actually raised by two families, which he says both contributed to the development of his career.

Chris's father, F.D. Reeve, has been quite successful during his career as a university professor and an author. Born in 1928 in Philadelphia, Pennsylvania, he graduated from Princeton University and received his Ph.D from Columbia University in 1958.

He has since received recognition as a poet, a novelist and a linguist. Aside from his native English, F.D. Reeve is also fluent in Russian and French. He accompanied poet Robert Frost on his 1962 trip to the Soviet Union. Reeve's assignment was to translate poet Frost's remarks for the benefit of Russian listeners during the tour. After this trip, F.D. Reeve published two books in 1964: *Robert Frost in Russia* and *The Russian Novel*. He also edited an anthology of Russian plays and Soviet short stories.

In 1969 Chris's famous father published a social novel *The Red Machines*. The author felt that he must experience first-hand the things he wrote about, so he became a character in his own story. The book described the lives of migrant farm workers who harvested wheat from Texas to South Dakota. The author took a job as a truck driver who carried the workers to the fields and back to their homes. He listened to them talk and learned how their lives were controlled by their work on the "red machines."

Actually, Chris's father, ever since his graduation from Princeton and Columbia, had tried many jobs before settling down to his present fame. First he was a longshoreman on the docks in New York City. Then he worked as a waiter. He even tried his hand at being an actor, but that didn't seem right for him. He did enjoy writing, though, and his poems were beginning to be published by *New York* and other widely read magazines.

Chris seems to have inherited a good deal of his father's creative talents. Many of the skills that make one a good writer also are necessary to be a good actor.

One Connecticut newspaper poked fun at F.D. Reeve when it ran this caption under his picture: "Marlon Brando plays a Wesleyan University teacher in a major Hollywood film? Not exactly, but Brando did play Superman's father. Christopher Reeve played Superman, and Reeve is the real-life son of Franklin D. Reeve, an adjunct professor at Wesleyan University in Middletown."

His father lives in Higganum, Connecticut, and teaches at Wesleyan as well as Yale University. He was busy preparing for a trip abroad when Chris's first big film was released. But he managed to find the time to see *Superman*, which he called "moderately good." He thought Chris did "very well," though.

What's interesting about Chris's past is that neither he nor his father watched much TV or ever read comic books. So when he was told the thrilling news about getting the part of Superman, the excited father ordered champagne to celebrate. He thought his son had a part in a well-known literary work of George Bernard Shaw, *Man and Superman*. Chris set him straight and everyone laughed about it. Defending him, Chris said: "From his background and experience, he wouldn't have thought that I'd be doing a comic book character."

Chris was born in Manhattan, but has not lived there all of his life. He spent the biggest part of his growing-up years living in Princeton, New Jersey, with his mother. She remarried to a stockbroker. His mother, Barbara Johnson, also has creative talent. She is a writer for *Town Topics*, a weekly Princeton publication.

Just after their divorce, his father moved to New Haven, Connecticut. Chris spent a great deal of time riding the railroad back and forth, so that he could spend time with both of his natural parents. He feels that both of them influenced his acting career. "My parents didn't shove," Chris recalls, "but they did encourage me to do what I wanted."

Chris was attracted to acting when he was about nine. By the time he reached thirteen he definitely wanted to be an actor. "The atmosphere around Princeton was perfect for my development. The McCarter Theater there was a great help and influence," he says.

When growing up, Chris was around important

people quite often. He remembers particularly that his mother had known President John F. Kennedy and other famous figures.

He feels lucky to have had what he considers "an extremely privileged background." The academic interests of his father helped Chris pursue a good education. He also says that there were people in his family who were wealthy. Chris insists, "I tried not to use it, but if I was in trouble, I knew there was money there, somewhere." One of the first things Chris did when he earned enough money from acting was to pay back his stepfather for his education.

Young people go through a difficult period of adolescence, trying to find out who they are and what they want to be. Luckily, Chris found his place in acting at an early age. He says that the theater saved him from a lot of growing-up problems. "Well, on Friday I'm down at the theater and I'm playing this part," Chris remembers. "I'm not me, I'm him—I'm the boy in *Our Town*. That got me through a lot of turmoil."

Other members of his family didn't find life quite so easy. Chris's brother, Benjamin, is slightly younger than he. Ben went through a difficult period in which frustration and anger about his parents' divorce and about growing up were hard for him to deal with. Chris tried to be understanding and helpful when Ben had problems in schools.

But now Benjamin is fine. He and Chris have remained best friends. Chris calls his brother a "part-time genius." At age thirteen, Ben invented a new computer programming language which was later taught at Princeton University. He's also a well-known architect and legal consultant. Chris is proud of his brother's skills and talent.

Ben took a whole building in New York City's Soho section—which has many run-down buildings—and rebuilt it beautifully.

Brother Benjamin is also a writer—although a different kind of writer than his father is. He has written books on the problems of energy, and now is trying a novel. And he has the skill of an accomplished photographer, too! Chris insists that his younger brother is "the extremely exceptional person in the Reeve family."

Chris and Ben look somewhat alike. They are both very casual in their appearance and in the way they dress. Chris boasts that even though he is famous he still "doesn't own a suit."

Ben has a loft apartment on the lower West Side of New York City. Chris often goes there to get away from his busy life-style. That is also where the actor goes to play his favorite Steinway grand piano which he was given at age sixteen.

Chris also has a half-sister, Allison, who is a medical student at the University of Connecticut; a half-brother, Mark, who is studying archeology at Harvard, and another half-brother, Brock, who is a Ph.D candidate in Classics at Yale.

Chris's family has been through a lot of changes through the years, but they've always been interested in each other's well-being. Since his parents were divorced during his childhood, he had an allegiance to both of them. But for many years they didn't speak to each other. Chris decided to try to end that situation with his Broadway debut. On opening night of *A Matter of Gravity* he got them all—his father and wife, and his mother and husband—tickets together in the same row. Chris was so pleased when they put aside past differences that night.

When Chris first got the part of Superman, some of his relatives feared that he would be too famous to have time to see them. But Chris insists that he treated his starring movie role just like he did any acting part. "It simply boils down to how you do the work," he said. Once the family understood Chris's attitude, they became more relaxed.

Occasionally his father would kid him about playing a "comic book" character, but the real problem was his mother. "I can't tell her anything about the movie without some risk; she's a newspaper reporter!," he laughs. When she would ask him for advance information for her newspaper, Chris would quiet her by saying: "Be a relative! You're my mother, not just a newspaper reporter. Let other people write the story."

V
Getting the Part

"I'm still stunned that, after the screen test and all the interviews, they've chosen me . . ."

The selection of Christopher Reeve ended a two-year search for the right actor to play the part of Superman. One of the biggest problems in casting the title role was the fact that so many people already had an idea in their heads of what the "Man of Steel" should look like. Not only would the star have to look like Superman, but he would also have to be able to speak and act.

The search began in 1975. Producer Ilya Salkind's first choice for the part was Robert Redford who was and continues to be a top box office draw. Attracted by Redford's acting ability, Salkind felt certain that makeup and costume would take care of the rest. But a Hollywood agent scoffed at the idea, saying that Redford wouldn't have made a believable Superman. Audiences might make such comments as "There's Robert Redford playing

Superman," and that wasn't what the producers had in mind. They wanted the actor to *be* Superman. Anyway, an agreement couldn't be reached on money and other issues, so Redford eventually turned down the part.

Paul Newman was also asked, but he turned down both the roles of Superman and Lex Luther. Although a very talented and popular actor, Newman probably wouldn't have been right for the part.

The producers got together and came up with a long list of names—everyone from well-known actors and professional athletes to many unknowns. And columnists in Hollywood had a playful time speculating who the star might be. Among those men considered and/or screen-tested were Steve McQueen, Charles Bronson, Warren Beatty, Sylvester Stallone, Clint Eastwood, Burt Reynolds, Ryan O'Neal, James Caan, Jon Voight, Robert Wagner, and Kris Kristofferson. A problem seemed to exist in every case—too busy, too heavy, too Italian, too old, too young, etc.

The key people in the project were getting desperate. Producer Salkind's wife's dentist was even screen-tested. But still no Superman. They had spent so much time, effort, and money and had failed. So they decided that they might be taking the wrong approach. Salkind thought that perhaps they shouldn't look for a well-known actor for the part. Besides, they already had a big name star—Marlon Brando—in the movie. He was under contract for nearly $4 million to play the role of Jor-El,

Superman's father. Shortly thereafter the producers signed another star, Gene Hackman, to play Lex Luther, the evil enemy of Superman. Hackman contracted for $2 million.

Now they were convinced that they should pursue a newcomer for the title role. First they tried athlete Bruce Jenner, but his screen test proved unsatisfactory. His "boyish" looks made him seem much too young on the screen. In addition, his lack of experience was also apparent in the test.

Stumped again, Salkind turned to the very large Academy Players Directory which contained photographs and summary credits of Screen Actors Guild members. He found some notes beside a picture which had previously been pointed out to him, and he decided to call the young actor.

Salkind found Christopher Reeve just returning from an audition for a Woolite commercial. Chris remembers, "My first reaction was poor Hollywood. How sad. Why can't they come up with something new and exciting?" But once he read the script he changed his mind.

Earlier the script had also been a problem, but by the time Chris was asked to read for the part, a team of top writers had worked on it. Mario Puzo (*The Godfather*), David and Leslie Newman (*Bonnie and Clyde*) and Robert Benton all had a hand in writing the screenplay.

Chris flew to London for his screen test, at Salkind's invitation, even though Director Dick Donner kept insisting that the actor—twenty-four at the time—was too young. Producer Pierre Spengler's wife was sent to greet him at the airport. Her immediate reaction to Chris was that he was perfect—and told her husband so without hesitation.

Donner's mind was changed, not by Mrs. Spengler though, but by Chris's screen test. The way he portrayed Clark Kent was exactly what they were looking for. He displayed just the right balance of bumbling and fumbling and innocence. And Chris looked perfect for the part dressed in a gray flannel suit with his hair slicked back and wearing horn-rimmed glasses. And when he was transformed into Superman, his fantastic acting ability enabled him to fit that part well, too. He appeared a gallant tower of strength as the "Man of Steel." He didn't look too young or too skinny, either.

Although the producers were quite certain they had found their Superman, they waited a while to make the announcement. So Chris went back to New York unsure if he had made it. On his way to the airport though, the studio's driver tried to reassure him, "I've seen nearly the whole lot of 'em . . . and you've got the part!"

Chris's agent got the news first when he heard Rona Barrett make the announcement on ABC-TV's "Good Morning, America." Then the producer called to confirm the story. Of course, Chris was excited. In an interview he said, "I'm still stunned that, after the screen test and all the interviews, they've chosen me. But somehow I feel ready for it; I feel I could fly—not literally, like Superman, but emotionally."

Aside from being chosen for his appearance and his acting ability, his newness to Hollywood seemed to be attractive to the producers. They felt that it would be easier to negotiate a contract with someone who wasn't a million-dollar superstar. Chris was paid the sum of $250,000 plus overtime for two-years' work. This may seem like a respectable starting salary for anyone, but it was small compared to the $4 million figure which was paid to Marlon Brando.

However, the producers contend that they were paying Chris a good salary for someone just beginning a motion picture career. They also said they planned to make more than one Superman picture, and Chris's salary would escalate with each one.

Aside from the amount of money he would earn, Chris still considered winning the role of Superman the opportunity of his life, and enthusiastically accepted it.

Chris began receiving all kinds of attention from star-watchers. On February 24, 1977, less than a month before the filming was scheduled to begin the *New York Times*'s "Notes on People" column ran the following article:

"That handsome young fellow getting all the attention at Sardi's Restaurant yesterday was Superman, or at least the movie's idea of the comic strip hero. He's 24-year-old Christopher Reeve, who won the coveted title role in the forthcoming $25 million film extravaganza after some two hundred young actors and others . . . had been tested. 'We wanted a relative unknown,' said the *Superman* director, Richard Donner, 'so the public wouldn't think of an established personality pretending he was flying and performing great feats of strength.' Mr. Reeve, who used to appear on the television soap opera "Love of Life," said that he had a pilot's license, 'but I don't think that's going to help much when I fly as Superman.' "

In another interview Director Donner declared, "If there's a God in heaven, he sent me Christopher Reeve."

As Superman, alias Clark Kent, Chris is actually playing two parts. And he has a certain philosophy about each character which helps him separate the two. "This is my wet look," he says, patting down his darkened brown hair. "Clark got stuck somewhere in the '60s. He's really Superman acting a schlepper and having a good time at it." Chris admits that the Clark Kent part of the role is not difficult for him. "I'm much more like Clark Kent," he says.

But although he didn't have to build Superman's character, Chris had to build up his physique.

The actor immediately rejected the option of having costume designers make his body appear more muscular by using Styrofoam falsies. Tall, but rather slender, when he got the part he was 6 feet 4 inches and weighed 188 pounds.

Chris jokes about how he put a Superman poster on the wall of his room and said, "That's what I must work up to." And work hard he did. He did strenuous exercises for two hours a day, six days a week under the direction of a trainer, plus he followed a very demanding eating schedule. Chris participated in rigorous daily workouts in what he recalls as a "sweaty, noisy London gym." His routine consisted of a series of limbering-up exercises, weightlifting, "pumping iron" and much grunting, sweating and panting. Chris did all of his exercises in combinations of three sets of ten each, and claims that "it's the third set that adds growth."

The actor added thirty pounds and increased his appetite tremendously. "The theory was to eat as much as you wanted—I was a joke in the dining room," Chris recalls. He was on a four-meal-a-day, high-protein diet.

Body builder David Prowse, who played Darth Vader in *Star Wars* was hired to supervise Chris's muscle-building campaign. Chris felt good after the workouts and was in excellent shape. He added some two inches to his chest and built up his strength considerably. His bench-pressing record rose from forty pounds to 320 pounds during the ten-week period. "By the time my body took shape I was able to loosen up," he says.

Even on the set, every now and then Chris would disappear to an empty corner of the stage. Ignoring the activity around him, he would do a few deep knee bends and stretching exercises to help keep him in shape for his difficult flying scenes.

As a result of the body-building program, Chris developed an enormous neck and shoulders. So in order to play each of his two roles effectively he had to move his body in different ways. When he was Superman he pulled himself upward, and with his hands confidently on his hips, he appeared to grow about three inches. When he was Clark Kent, he took on a slouching posture, dropping his shoulders and curling his spine.

"How you carry yourself is ninety percent of the initial impression you make on other people. The other ten percent is mental attitude," he says. Chris interprets Superman's feeling as one of relaxed control; and Clark's as being like a puppet.

Chris doesn't mind the costumes too much and he does wear the traditional Clark Kent glasses and Superman cape. He doesn't like to use makeup, although he does when necessary. "People want to see Superman a certain way and you have to honor that expectation. So I give them that and then take it one step further with Clark Kent. We take away the makeup that strengthens Superman's features. I shrink—Clark actually walks about three inches shorter than Superman. My voice becomes flatter, more Midwestern—Clark has asthma. It's putting the two halves together that's the challenge," he said.

VI
Where Did Superman
Come From?

"He's [Superman] an orphan, and that governs his emotional behavior; and he's an alien, and what makes him super is he's got the wisdom to use his powers well."

Now we know how Christopher Reeve got to be Superman. But some people may be wondering where Superman came from.

Superman was born in Cleveland, Ohio, not on the mysterious planet of Krypton. He was the creation of two high school students named Jerry Siegel and Joe Shuster. The late 1920s and early 1930s, often called The Depression Era, was a period when people needed a hero. Times were hard and many people were poor and unemployed. The legend of Superman helped raise the morale of people who were so troubled.

The actual year of Superman's first appearance

was 1933. Jerry Siegel was a creative teenager who attended Glenville High School and worked on a magazine called *Science Fiction*. He was an avid reader of short stories and science fiction. Combining some ideas and character types which particularly appealed to him, Siegal created a new character which was different and more advanced than any that had ever been written about. Discussing his character, Siegel said, "All of a sudden it hits me. I conceived a character like Samson, Hercules and all the strong men I ever heard of rolled into one. Only more so."

Siegel enthusiastically shared his idea with his friend Joe Shuster, who was an amateur illustrator. Equally excited about the character, Shuster created some sketches of the superhero with no difficulty at all.

Both boys were shy kids, but they fantasized about what they would like to be. Clark Kent was modeled after Joe, who always wore glasses. Lois Lane was inspired by a friend named Joanne Carter, who later married Jerry.

Like all budding young writers, the two young men encountered some difficulty in having their stories published. But finally in 1935, two years after they first began working on their idea, they secured jobs with the company now known as D.C. Comics.

In June 1938, Superman burst upon the world in the first issue of Action Comics. Back then a copy of the famous comic cost only 10 cents. Today, anyone lucky enough to have one of the originals could probably get five thousand dollars for it. That's just one indication of how popular Superman has become.

Since his introduction, Superman, also known as the "Man of Steel", has been considered the world's mightiest adventure hero. He has gained more fame and popularity than his creators ever imagined he would.

Compared with the powers he possesses today—those exhibited by Chris Reeve in the *Superman* movie—the powers of the original hero in the comic strip were very modest. For example, the first edition of Action Comics claimed that Superman could "leap one-eighth of a mile; hurdle a twenty-story building . . . raise tremendous weights . . . run faster than an express train . . . and that nothing less than a bursting shell could penetrate his skin!"

Over the years, however, the writers of Superman comics and scripts have updated his powers and made him perform more thrilling and exciting challenges. Today, the "Man of Steel" can withstand the heat at the core of the sun, fly through the air faster than the speed of light, peer through walls with his X-ray vision, and hurl entire planets across the length of the universe. But the writers have not allowed Superman to abuse his powers.

From the very beginning, Superman continually grew in popularity. First, the length of the comic book stories was increased. Then, in February 1940, a radio program was introduced. Broadcast three times a week, it became one of the most listened-to programs on the air. Well-known sportscaster of today, Bud Collier, was the voice of Superman, Joan Alexander was Lois Lane and Julian Noa was Perry White.

The popularity of the radio show led to the writing of a book by George Lowther in 1942. A *Superman* serial produced by Columbia Pictures marked the next appearance of the superhero. Kirk Alyn starred as Superman in two fifteen-episode feature length films. Actress Noel Neill played the role of Lois Lane.

These two actors have enjoyed a long association with Superman. A little too old now to play their original roles, they do have bit parts in the new *Superman* movie. They play the roles of young Lois Lane's parents. Their scene in the current movie takes place during the period of Superman's boyhood. The camera zooms in to show the Lane family enjoying a moment of conversation as the train on which they are travelling passes through Smallville. Young Lois is gazing out the window and catches a momentary glimpse of young Clark Kent racing across the countryside, actually running faster than the train. (Often in movies and plays this technique called *foreshadowing* is used to help give the audience a hint about what's coming in the story.)

After the success of the serials of 1950, the same studio produced a film starring George Reeves as Superman and Phyllis Coates as Lois Lane. With the appearance of televisions in millions of homes,

Superman was brought to an increasing number of people. The famed TV series began in 1951 and continued until 1957, although reruns have been aired many times since the actual production of episodes stopped. The TV cast included movie star George Reeves (no relation to Christopher—although as a child Chris often wished he could claim association) as Superman and the original Lois, Noel Neill. Other members of what came to be known as the "Superman family" included Jack Larson as Jimmy Olsen, John Hamilton as Perry White and Robert Shayne as Inspector Henderson.

Another extension of the original story was a successful Broadway musical in 1966 with the familiar title "It's a Bird . . . It's a Plane . . . It's Superman!" Robert Benton and David and Leslie Newman, the writers of that play, also maintained their association with Superman. They were among the people who worked on the screenplay for the movie *Superman*.

The two people who were responsible for the creation of Superman some 45 years ago are still around today. Anyone would think that Jerry Siegel and Joe Shuster, both 64, would be extremely happy about the popularity of their character. But they're not. Earlier in their careers, they signed a standard contract with the comic company, losing their copyright and becoming strictly employees of the firm. They never made a penny from the movie serial or the TV series. Finally, they brought a lawsuit against the comic book company for renewal of their copyright. Even though they lost the suit, hundreds of sympathic letters were sent to Warner Communications, the company which had since bought out D.C. Comics. The two men, in failing health, were finally awarded a lifetime annual income of $20 thousand each plus medical benefits from the company.

Both are delighted to see the success of their creation, but feel left out and forgotten. They were, however, invited to attend *Superman* premiers in New York, Washington and Los Angeles as Warner's guests. They both loved the movie. Excited about seeing their creation on the screen, they insisted that Chris Reeve has just the right touch of humor. "He really *is* Superman," they said. But still sad about the past, Joe added, "We would love to have been consultants on the movie. If they ever want any help on the sequel, they know where to find us."

And what does Chris think about Superman, the character that has made him so famous? Not having been an avid fan of either the Superman comics or TV series, Chris has recently grown to understand the character well. Before they started filming, he met with some of the comic book writers. They told him to remember two important things about Superman which, he says, helped him greatly in his acting of the role. "He's an orphan, and that governs his emotional behavior; and he's an alien, and what makes him super is he's got the wisdom to use his power well." Chris feels that the "Man of Steel" bit is too exaggerated and that he only has super powers because he's from another planet.

Chris insists that if Superman had grown up on Krypton where he was born he might have been an ordinary person, like a plumber. But on Earth, he's a fantasy. Knowing all this helps Chris put the role in the proper perspective and enables him to separate Superman from Clark Kent.

VII
Making the Movie *Superman*

"A lot's at stake for me in this film."

With the excitement still high about finding Chris Reeve to play Superman, the producers had to go back to work to find a Lois Lane. They were most anxious about this task since filming was planned to begin in less than a month.

Several top name female stars had already been cast for the film. Actress Susannah York was contracted to play opposite star Marlon Brando as Superman's mother. English star Sara Douglas was to play Ursa of the planet Krypton. Valerine Perrine, well-known for her role as Honey Bruce opposite Dustin Hoffman in the film *Lenny*, was cast as the villainess, Eve Teschmacher.

Tom Mankiewicz had been working in Los Angeles as a creative consultant to the *Superman* director. He suggested the name of an actress whose talent he felt had not been recognized by the producers. Margot Kidder was at home on her Montana ranch when they called and asked her to read for the part of Lois Lane.

Her first reaction was similar to that of Chris Reeve when he was first asked to be in *Superman*. "What is this, some kind of a joke or something?" she replied. But after reading the script, she, too, became enthusiastic about the movie. And she was extremely pleased to get the part.

Margot claims that although she had heard of Superman while she was growing up in Canada, like Chris Reeve, she had never read the comic strip. Someone gave her her first Superman comic book the day before her screen test.

With all of the starring roles and most of the other parts cast, the filming could begin. March 29, 1977 was the first full day of main unit shooting. The space used for this part of the filming was in Shepperton Studios in England. Recently, most of Shepperton was purchased by the Who, a well-known British rock group. They wanted to use the space as a recording studio. The part being used to film *Superman* was small compared to some Hollywood studios.

The filming of *Superman* took more than 350 actual shooting days. Reportedly some $50 million was spent on the combined effort of making *Superman* and part of *Superman II*. A record amount of 1,250,000 feet of film was shot, of which only about twelve thousand feet would become part of the finished movie. (Compared to only 400,000 feet shot for *Jaws* and 800,000 for *A Bridge Too Far*—both films thought to have been extravagant when they were made.) Some one thousand people including actors, technicians, makeup and costume artists, set designers and other crew members were employed. The filming took place in three different studios on three continents of the world and in a total of eight countries. Now that was quite a production!

Chris maintained his cool sense of humor and personality both on and off the set. One of the scenes in New York was filmed at the Solow Building, a modern skyscraper structure on West 57th Street. This being his first public appearance as "The Man of Steel" in New York, he was understandably nervous. After changing into his famous costume, Chris was attached to the flying rig and hoisted up into the darkened night sky. Suddenly there was lots of enthusiastic cheering and applause from the crowd. Despite his touch of "stage fright," Chris broke into a huge smile and waved back at the crowd.

Later on that very same week, Chris was filming a scene in Brooklyn, New York. During rehearsals of the flying scenes, to the onlookers' delight, Superman was seen high above the buildings eating a banana.

Being the modest person that he is, Chris didn't like to be recognized as Superman in public. But some members of the flying unit decided to have some fun one day just as Chris was on his way back to New York for the Christmas holidays. They called the departure lounge at Heathrow Airport in London and had an airline employee page Superman and remind him to keep his arms straight while flying. Chris was terribly embarrassed but nonetheless laughed at the joke. And from that day on his arms were always in the proper position for flying.

Every movie has its catastrophes and funny stories about things that happened during the filming. And *Superman* has its share. One in particular took place about a week after filming began in New York. The cast and crew took over the New York *Daily News* building on East 42nd Street in the big city. By changing the sign outside, the building was transformed into Perry White's *Daily Planet* offices. As if to prove that Superman did indeed have power, the "Great Blackout of 1977" hit New York City. A huge electrical storm had knocked out all electricity. For almost twenty-six hours, most of the city was without power. That is, except for the *Daily Planet* (*Daily News*) building. The filming was stopped, and the movie company moved its giant generator-powered lights inside the building. Although the presses couldn't operate, the *Daily News* building was the only building in New York City with its lights on.

Despite the numerous unexpected problems and delays, many of the scenes from *Superman II* have already been filmed. In the sequel, the original three villains come back to attack Earth. They invade the White House, rough up the President (who is played by E.G. Marshall), destroy Metropolis and end up running the whole world. And Superman decides to relinquish his super powers in favor of his love for Lois Lane. It is scheduled to be released in June 1981.

Actors learn from each other. And while working on *Superman*, Chris associated with many top names and highly experienced people. He shared the set with many of them. But some were never on camera during any of his scenes. Nevertheless, Chris made it a point of getting to know as many of the actors as possible.

"A lot's at stake for me in this film," he said. And he decided to take advantage of the opportunity to improve and develop his acting skills that will help him in his future career.

To him, one of the most important of the stars was Marlon Brando. He arrived on the set just a few days after completing filming of the difficult role he played in *Apocolypse Now*. Brando was tired and run-down from his previous hard work and he had a bad cold. But nonetheless he maintained his professional attitude and met his call sheet schedule.

The day filming began was the first time Chris had the opportunity to get acquainted with Marlon Brando. Chris had long been looking forward to their meeting. When he first landed the Superman part he said, "In addition to the possibility that this will be my chance of a lifetime to become a movie star, I'm going to have the privilege of working with the greatest actor of our time, Marlon Brando. He's playing my father."

The young actor received a very warm welcome from Mr. Brando. Chris didn't quite know what to expect, but the great actor came right over to him, introduced himself and said that he was glad they would be working together. When Chris returned to his dressing room he discovered an expensive basket of champagne and caviar waiting for him. The attached handwritten note from Brando wished Chris good luck in the film and in his career. At several times during the movie, Brando took a special interest in the young actor's career and made himself available to give Chris advice about his future.

During the filming of *Superman*, Chris watched Marlon Brando's actions on the set very carefully. The young actor was amazed to see that Brando's lines were displayed on large boards in front of the set for each take. When asked the reason for this, Brando told Chris about his belief that memorizing lines takes something away from the effectiveness of an actor's performance. He said that with a quick reading of the cue cards he can be more natural in both speaking and acting, and have more time to actually think about what he as the character should be doing.

Chris found a lot of humor in the personality of his co-star Margot Kidder. He fondly remembers that when she was told she had won the part of Lois Lane, she rushed off to an exclusive shop to buy some fancy clothing that she had been wanting.

Chris and others of the *Superman* cast were anxiously waiting to meet Gene Hackman when he arrived on the set. But they were forewarned that he was a very private person. Also, his time during his first few days was taken up being fitted for all of the crazy costumes and wigs he would be wearing in the movie.

Chris enjoyed getting to know actress Valerie Perrine who's bubbly and has a very outgoing personality. Valerie arrived the first day with her small group of friends and immediately made the rounds of the studio getting acquainted with everyone. She also arranged a luncheon to help her get to know some of the cast and crew, including Chris of course.

Chris did not share any scenes with well-known Glenn Ford who played Jonathan Kent in the movie. The role of young Clark Kent was played by Jeff East, and Chris didn't enter the movie until after Superman's Earth father, Jonathan Kent, had died.

But Chris admired Glenn Ford for his long and varied career. Ford got his first taste of acting at the young age of four. He claims that in the small role he played back then he had to eat a large dish of ice cream.

Ned Beatty and Christopher Reeve had crossed paths before *Superman*. The two had acted together in the disaster movie, *Gray Lady Down*.

Playing the part of Otis in *Superman* was quite different from the dramatic sort of roles with which Beatty had previously been associated. He appeared in *Deliverance*, *Promises in the Dark*, *All the President's Men*, and received an Academy Award nomination as Best Supporting Actor in *Network*.

He has appeared on such well-known TV series as "The Waltons," "Gunsmoke," and "The Rockford Files," and received high acclaim for his performance in the TV special movie, "Friendly Fire."

Much of the success of a movie can be attributed to its director. It's his vision and expertise that makes it all hang together. The director must coordinate all aspects of the movie including the sets, the costumes, the camera crew, the actors, the special effects and the screenplay.

And Christopher Reeve has Richard Donner to thank for the way *Superman* turned out. Because of Donner's skillful directing, Chris became a superstar.

Donner's interpretation of the movie *Superman* presents it as actually three movies in one. The first story begins on the planet Krypton with a science-fiction-like treatment of the story of Superman's infancy. The second sequence takes place in Kansas farm country where baby Superman becomes Clark Kent, the child of two Earth parents, Ma and Pa Kent. Before the beginning of the third section of the movie, the audience is briefly reminded of Superman's past via a visit to the North Pole. Here Superman communicates with the image of his Kryptonian father, Jor-El. The action then switches to Metropolis, a practically undisguised New York City, where Chris Reeve begins his role as Clark Kent. This part of the movie introduces all of the legendary familiar characters from the original comic strip. Thus Director Donner has carefully woven all the elements of the Superman story together.

The director auditioned some three hundred actors for the title role before selecting Christopher Reeve. When Chris read for the part, Donner realized he didn't have to look any further. "Physically, nobody could look more perfect for the role. One of the biggest problems lies in portraying the difference between Clark Kent and Superman. You can change their attire, but the actor has to find the distinction between the characters and keep his identity while in conflict with himself. It's phenomenal to see the changes the kid goes through!" the director remarks. Donner admits that he can take only a minimum amount of credit for Chris's outstanding performance in the movie.

Another person for whom Chris has a great deal of respect and gratitude is the casting director— Mr. Lynn Stalmaster. The casting director in a movie, play or show is the person who works with the show's director to cast every speaking role, negotiates with agents on salary and billing, makes sure the actor is in good standing with the Screen Actors' Guild, and performs a variety of valuable services to both the actor and the show's company.

Christopher Reeve owes his first opportunity to Stalmaster, who cast him in the bit part as a naval officer in *Gray Lady Down*. A list of some other films cast by the "Master Caster" show just how many budding actors like Chris were given their start in small roles, and went on to become major actors: Jon Voight spoke only four lines in *Hour of the Gun*, Richard Dreyfuss had one line in *The Graduate*, James Caan appeared but did not speak in *Irma La Douce*, Gilda Radner appeared in a party scene in *The Last Detail*.

Stalmaster works hard for the actors as well as for the directors and producers who buy his services. He tries to relax the actors and prepare them for their big appearance before the director by providing them with scripts, reading practice and even coaching on their physical appearance.

The first thing that impressed Chris about Lynn Stalmaster was his Hawaiian shirt. Chris recalls, "He used to come into New York in the middle of the winter, and we'd all walk in with boots and coats and umbrellas. He would be sitting in his hotel room wearing lightweight pants, white shoes, and a Hawaiian shirt."

This gave Chris a feeling that Stalmaster was a visitor from a wonderful land. He represented hope and opportunity for the young actor. "An appointment with Lynn Stalmaster was considered very good luck—fortune smiled on you for a moment," Chris says.

Despite some fatherly advice from veteran actor Marlon Brando, Chris did all of his own stunt work. Brando said, "It's not worth risking your life for—it's only a movie." Chris was adamant about playing the entire role of "The Man of Steel".

Special effects director Colin Chilvers credits the technical crew with finally coming up with a believable way to make Superman fly. They used a few basic techniques. One was a complex network of wires attached to a hydraulic system of tracks and pulleys. There was also a pole-arm, a fourteen-foot boom that was attached to Superman for such sequences as his flight over Metropolis with Lois Lane. During this beautifully romantic scene, however, the apparatus began to crack. Margot Kidder began to get nervous uttering the words, "Oh, God, get us out of here." Chris recalls reaching out his hand to catch her in his Superman frame of mind. "When I get in the costume something takes over," he says.

Many of the crew credited Chris with being much more coordinated than many of the acrobats and stunt people they had originally considered using. Actually, he had already learned to fly before his courageous and convincing stunt work in the movies. He owns a glider and is a licensed pilot. Chris didn't credit his plane-flying ability with making him able to fly as Superman. It did, however, help overcome what other actors might have —fear of heights.

Also, Chris realized that his success as Superman depended upon the believability of the flying scenes. So he spent a good deal of time in the air, often suspended thirty feet over the studio on the pole-arm rig.

Even though he often flies his plane over water, Chris didn't particularly enjoy dangling 240 feet over Manhattan's East River suspended from a crane. "With my little red boots limp like spinach, I wouldn't do that again," shudders Chris.

A very cooperative actor, Chris complained very little about all the time it took to film some of the difficult scenes. "The flying is all me," he boasts. "It's not a bunch of midgets." At some points during the shooting he was two hundred feet off the ground in the bitter cold. When asked if it bothered him Chris would reply that after the first fifty feet it didn't make any difference to him.

Chris Reeve flashing his super smile! *Photo by Tony Rizzo*

Chris with Margot Kidder, who played the role of Lois Lane in *Superman*. *Photo by Globe Photos*

Chris poses as Superman against the scenic Manhattan sky-
line. *Wide World Photos*

Logan Fleming, sculptor and art director for the Stars Hall of Fame in Orlando, Florida, creates a wax likeness of Chris Reeve as Superman. *Photo by Globe Photos*

In this scene from *Superman*, Clark Kent is able to exhibit his super powers by catching a bullet and saving Lois Lane from muggers. *Wide World Photos*

Chris as the "mild mannered reporter," Clark Kent. *Photo by Bob Deutsch/Globe Photos*

Chris appeared at the West Coast premiere of *Superman* with co-star Margot Kidder. *Wide World Photos*

Gene Hackman, (right) plays Lex Luthor Superman's archenemy. *Wide World Photos*

Chris at his "hole-in-the-wall" apartment in New York. *Photo by Tony Rizzo*

Chris likes to keep his fans happy. He's always eager to sign autographs. *Photo by Bob Deutsch*

Photo by Donald Sanders/Globe Photos

Casually dressed and sporting that unforgettable smile, Chris Reeve is undeniably a superstar. *Photo by Bob Deutsch*

Chris was photographed with Gae Exton at a press party for *Superman. Photo by Nate Cutler/Globe Photos*

Here, Chris chats with co-workers between rehearsals for the play *Fifth of July*. (Left to right: director, Marshall Mason, Swoosie Kurtz, Chris Reeve, and playwright Lanford Wilson). *Wide World Photos*

In a more dramatic role, Chris starred with Jane Seymour in *Somewhere in Time*. *Wide World Photos*

Backstage at the Uris Theater, Chris met actress Angela Lansbury who originally starred in *Sweeney Todd. Wide World Photos*

VIII
Will the Real Lois Lane Please Stand Up?

"It (acting) was great fun. You got to drink cokes and eat chocolate bars, and laugh it up a lot."

Christopher Reeve is not the only actor who received a big break in his career by being cast in *Superman*. Margot Kidder gained much notoriety and respect as an actress for her portrayal of Lois Lane in the movie. The huge attendance which the film enjoyed gave new solidity to the young woman's career, which had previously seemed not so promising.

Unlike the case of Christopher Reeve however, Margot's interest in acting began somewhat later in life. Born in Yellowknife, Canada, a small frostbitten town on the North Shore of Great Slave Lake in the Northwest Territories, Margot led a rather sheltered life. She is the daughter of a mining engineer, and lived the first two and a half years of her life in a caboose. She didn't have much opportunity to see movies or experience live theater. But Margot was an avid reader of movie magazines. "I had to sneak them into the house because they were not considered appropriate reading material for a young girl," Margot recalls. Reading about the movies helped her dream and imagine herself in all kinds of situations. Margot says that she enjoyed an enormous fantasy life, which probably helped her develop some of the creative skills she now uses in acting roles.

By the age of twelve, Margot had developed the idea that she might want to become an actress. Since the small isolated community in which she lived offered little opportunity to develop acting skills, at age seventeen Margot left home to pursue her life's ambition. Having little experience, the main assets she possessed were self-sufficency and the obsession with becoming an actress.

Margot insists that she sought an acting career, not because she had a great desire to act, but because she was introduced to the profession by someone she knew. Actually, she was originally chasing after a boyfriend who she thought could help her find a career. She was lured into playing a role in a college production of "Take Me Along." Margot recalls, "It was great fun. You got to drink cokes and eat chocolate bars, and laugh it up a lot." In addition to having a good time, she learned some acting skill as well. Margot developed the unique ability to cry on cue. She felt that if she could do that while still seeming natural, she had it made as an actress. But later she discovered that there was much more technique involved in acting, and that she still had a lot to learn. After she and the boyfriend split, Margot quickly developed the attitude that whatever it was she wanted out of life, she would have to get for herself.

They had reached Toronto. Losing her friend there was actually lucky for Margot. On her own and quite by accident, she landed a job acting for the Canadian Broadcasting Company. Margot's flirtatious and zany personality, as well as her innocence, helped her get the job. She became the house actress who was cast in a number of small roles calling for a naive young woman. Once again Margot was called upon to use her ability to cry on cue. The roles she played included a crazy girl who liked to kill things, as well as a mixed up teenager.

The job didn't pay much though. So in order to earn the money she needed to live, Margot had to also wait on tables at a restaurant, sell hairnets in a beauty supply store, and moniter equipment at a figure salon. She recalls that the part she hated the most was "strapping fat ladies to vibrating machines."

Margot stayed in Toronto for about two years before finding her way to the movie capital of the world—Hollywood. One day, when she least expected it, Margot got a call from a Hollywood agent. She borrowed four hundred and fifty dollars and bought an airline ticket to the city that she hoped would bring her closer to her dream. "Why not?" she asked herself. "It seemed like a marvelous way to make a living."

Her beginnings in Hollywood included a year as a film editor before getting any acting roles. During this time she learned all about movie people, how they think, the special Hollywood language they speak, and how to get along in the film industry.

She finally got her first role in 1969. She played the high-class leading character in the movie *Gaily, Gaily*. Next, she landed a part in the British movie *Quackser Fortune Has a Cousin in the Bronx*, where she met and adored the star Gene Wilder. The well-known actor helped her realize that there was more to acting than simply crying on cue. He also cautioned her to learn to resist the manipulation of her career by strong actors and directors.

At first Margot was scared by the whole situation. She was her own self critic and felt that she wasn't doing a good enough acting job. To her surprise, though, Margot got good reviews from the critics. Her reaction to these were: "It made me more certain than ever that reviewers don't know what they're talking about."

Margot didn't consider this whole experience very successful. In addition, she grew to hate the director with whom she was working. At the Cannes Festival in France where the film was being shown, Margot realized her disenchantment with the whole scene. "Is this what life's really like?" she questioned.

Although she was doing quite well, Margot was becoming discouraged with the quality of her life in

Hollywood. In addition to disliking some of the people, she hated living in a hotel, and most nights ended up crying herself to sleep because of her loneliness. Some actors might choose to stick out such an uncomfortable situation, but not Margot. She decided to return to Canada for a while to engage in further formal acting studies.

Paying a little more attention to her future upon her return to her country, Margot bought a piece of land with a small house by a lake. Here she could relax and reflect on her work. Also she began to teach film editing with the idea of helping others practice and apply some of the techniques she had studied.

But again, Margot ran out of money and turned back to acting for a chance to earn some funds. She reluctantly accepted a part in a film series called *Nicholas*, but feared the series might turn out to be a flop. Working with James Garner on this project actually turned out to be one of the best working experiences she ever had.

She again proved her sharpness and talent by making a TV mini-movie with star Hal Holbrook called *Suddenly Single*. As expected, the project was very successful. This film helped give Margot more confidence than ever, and she was able to return to full career status pursuing Hollywood roles.

Her outstanding movie credits have included "Mod Squad" (episode, 1970), "The Bounty Map" (episode, 1972), "Banacek" (episode, 1973), "Barnaby Jones" (episode, 1973), "Honky Tonk" (a film, 1974), "Baretta" (episode, 1975), and

"Switch" (episode, 1976).

Some of her major Motion Pictures roles prior to landing the part of Lois Lane included *Blood Sisters, The Gravy Train, Quiet Days in Belfast, The Great Waldo Pepper, The Reincarnation of Peter Proud, 92 in the Shade,* and *Santa Fe* 1836.

While acting in films, Margot also became a member of the women's workshop at the American Film Institute. This gave her the opportunity to apply her many other talents in writing and directing a short feature length film called *Again*.

Just as before, her personal life crept in to interfere with her career. "I kept falling in love and dumping my career," Margot commented. This time "Mr. Right" was Tom McGuane, novelist/screenwriter who she met while starring in *92 in the Shade*. Off she went to join him on his three hundred acre ranch in Montana to cook her favorite foods, ride horses, and live a relaxed life.

Being a housewife on the ranch just didn't seem to work out for Margot, though, and she and Tom were divorced after only a few years. However, Margot insists that something good came out of their relationship—she gave birth to a baby girl named Maggie. "The happiest day of my life was the day she was born," Margot says.

Now Margot's favorite pastime, in addition to being an actress, is being a mother. She takes Maggie along wherever she can. Even when she is not nearby, Margot still wears her daughter's tiny gold bracelet as a token of her love on a chain around her neck. "The minute I had Maggie, I just knew

I'd done something wonderful. It's just like being in love twenty-four hours a day . . . For a time I was frantic to try everything and a lot of that was a search for what I found when I gave birth to Maggie," philosophizes the actress.

With her personal life looking more positive, Margot's career also took a good turn when she won the coveted role of Lois Lane in *Superman*. As she flew off to the audition, she had serious doubts about what she was doing. "I thought, no way I'm gonna get this part," recalls Margot. But she was pleasantly surprised when she flew to London, screen tested on Thursday, got the part on Friday, and began filming on Monday. "The whole experience was such a jolt," she says. "It was disorienting. I was in a panic when we began shooting."

It was a difficult movie to make with all of the locations and special effects, which sometimes didn't work. But she and Christopher Reeve hit it off so well. Margot calls them "blood relations." As an actress, Margot rarely does the same thing the same way twice. Chris, on the other hand is very precise. Often on the set they would have to carefully plan their actions prior to filming a scene, just so that they would each know what to expect from the other. In spite of their artistic differences, though, they get along famously and make a great team of stars.

When not involved in the scene being filmed on the *Superman* set, Margot spent a great deal of time entertaining and amusing people. She was often found clowning around. Chris remembers laughing at her and Jack O'Halloran (who played a villian on Krypton) dancing and singing, running all over the set and jumping off the glacier-like structures of the Fortress of Solitude.

On the screen, Margot is just as playful. One reporter wrote this about her: "She's bouncy, has a wacky sense of humor, is always wisecracking and absolutely self-confident."

Although on the set she wears very fashionable business-like clothes in her portrayal of Lois Lane, Margot's personal style is a very casual one. Somewhat like Christopher Reeve, Margot enjoys comfortable attire. Her favorite outfits include tie-dyed T-shirts, drawstring pants, and cork-soled clogs. Even though she's been tremendously successful as a result of her part in *Superman*, she still drives a beat-up used Buick with banana milkshakes and orange crush spilled all over the seats. She plans to spend part of her time in her home in Malibu doing "ordinary things" like growing vegetables, reading and writing. And, she refuses to get a swimming pool because she thinks its "too California." She also maintains an apartment in New York so that she can spend time with her boyfriend John Heard, who has a career in the theater.

Margot is young and her career has really only just begun. When asked what she'd like to do next she says, "I had great directing ambitions, . . . but directing would mean I'd have to drop out of mothering. Another acting job would do fine." But she insists that she wants to do something meaningful with her life besides just making money. After her success in *Superman*, Margot will probably have the opportunity to pursue any kind of role or other film related job she wishes.

IX
The Selling of Superman

"He heard it was formal, and as you know, he has only one suit."

All you have to do is visit any store in the country, or for that matter, in the world to see the wide range effects of Superman. The well-known character was introduced in 1938 in the first issue of Action Comics. Since then he has been the hero supreme in comic books, TV shows, toys and games, and now in the movies. The legend of Superman is a world-wide phenomenon. Stories are published in eight different comic magazines which are available in thirty-eight countries and in fifteen languages.

As the budget for the making of *Superman*, rose, so did the public's interest in the film and in its main character. "Supermania," as it is called, was enhanced by the merchandising efforts of the movie's producers. All kinds of items about the movie and bearing the Superman logo were available: toys, T-shirts, watches, records, posters, paper products, party goods, clothing, sheets and towels to name just a few. The red-and-yellow Superman "S" could be seen in the most unusual places—the backsides of jeans, the rear door of "funky" cars, in airplanes and subway cars, and even on underwear. A poster of Chris Reeve both as Superman and as himself has a prominent place on many a wall in the homes of young people everywhere. Superman references are even on popular magazine covers. Aside from the movie's Chris Reeve himself, super "Henry the K" (Kissinger) and actress Barbra Streisand in a Superman T-shirt were among those photographed.

Warner Books, part of the same parent company as the film-maker, put out several new Superman-related titles at the time of the movie. They included a novelization of the screenplay, *The Making of Superman, The Great Superman Book, The Superman Blueprints, The Official Superman Quiz Book, The Superman Portfolio, the 1979 Superman Calendar* and a *Superman Scrapbook*.

D.C. Comics, which had been taken over by Warner Brothers some 10 years before, publicized the film in *The Superman Book*, twenty-eight other comic books, and in its thirty-five million reader daily newspaper comic strip. They even ran a contest open to all readers of D.C. Comic Books.

Star Christopher Reeve, Publisher Jenette Kahn, and D.C. Comics President Sol Harrison all participated in selecting the winners. The judges had to wade through some super-sized stacks of mail to select the lucky entries. The contest involved clipping letters of the alphabet from D.C. Comic Books to spell out the names SUPERMAN, KAL-EL, and CLARK. Tens of thousands of entries came in from Canada, Europe and all over the United States.

Two first-prize winners were selected at random. The two boys—Tim Hussey of California and Ed Finneran of Massachusetts—received several wonderful prizes. First they went on a free trip to New York where they had a VIP tour of the D.C. Comics offices. Then they were flown to Calgary, Alberta, Canada, where one of the movie's scenes was being shot. The two appeared in the movie as members of the Smallville High School football team. The scene was one about Superman's growing-up years on the Midwestern farm.

The advertising campaign to sell the movie was also carefully planned. Tops in the media field, Stephen O. Frankfurt of Frankfurt Communications, Inc., was selected for the job. He decided to take a low-key approach to the ads. "The problem" he explained, "is that Superman is so well-known world-wide people may discount the movie . . ." And although there were some very famous members of the cast like Marlon Brando and Gene Hackman, the title role was played by unknown Christopher Reeve. In addition, Frankfurt considered another important fact. "Millions of people have their own image of Superman, and we realized that all we'd have to tell them is that the movie is coming."

The first ad appeared as a full-color, two-page spread in the December 1978 issue of *Life* Magazine. It was a close-up shot of Clark Kent's shirt opening up to show the symbolic "S." The copy read simply, "The movie is coming for Christmas."

Actor Chris Reeve didn't get very involved in advertising decisions. However, one aspect of the merchandising and licensing agreements concerned him. Some of the manufacturers who purchased the rights to produce Superman-related items wanted to change their original agreement. They held the right to use the cartoon character but now wanted to use the likeness of actor Reeve in their Superman products.

The movie opened in December 1978 with old fashioned star-studded world premiere celebrations in several cities across the country. The first of these took place in Washington D.C. The event was first-class all the way—with black ties, formal attire, limousines and even a few laser beams seen in the night sky.

"Superman, more powerful than a locomotive and faster than a speeding bullet, has been used to sell everything from bonds during World War II to physical fitness during the Kennedy Administration. But this time he soared over buildings, turned back time to revive Lois Lane, saved California and vanquished an assortment of villians to benefit the International Special Olympics, an athletic program for the mentally and physically handicapped that was started by Eunice Kennedy Shriver ten years ago," wrote *The New York Times*.

The three-day gathering to raise money for the Special Olympics collected some $200,000 for the program. There were hundreds of guests at the event including former President and Mrs. Carter, TV news personality Barbara Walters, news commentator Roger Mudd, the famous soccer star Pele, Mr. and Mrs. Henry Kissinger, the chairman of Warner Communications (the company which produced the movie) Steve Ross, and, of course, the movie's star, Christopher Reeve.

When introduced in front of the audience, Chris apologized to the crowd for the absence of the "Man of Steel." "He heard it was formal, and as you know, he has only one suit," he teased. The crowd broke into laughter.

The next day some 1,300 were present at the second premiere showing of *Superman*. It too was a glamorous affair. This one, however, had new faces and different VIP's. New York Governor Carey was accompanied by his three children, all of whom were celebrating birthdays. Among the notables attending were: TV host Dick Cavett, tennis star Vitas Gerulaitis, Broadway star Tammy Grimes, "Saturday Night Live's" Gilda Radner, composer Alan Jay Lerner and an assortment of members of the Kennedy clan. There were all different kinds of people all interested in seeing *Superman*. Some remembered having watched him on television, and were excited about seeing the modern-day version.

Chris attended this extravaganza, too, and so did his co-star, Margot Kidder. She was dressed quite unlike reporter Lois Lane who she portrays in the movie. Ms. Kidder's elegant floor-length white coat attracted the eyes of many in the crowd.

Several guests were wearing attention-getting Superman-like clothing. Such articles as red and gold T-shirts, long-flowing capes, and jackets with the Superman logo were noticed. Author Mario Puzo, who worked on the *Superman* screenplay, wore a specially designed blue Superman T-shirt bearing a big gold "S" in the middle.

In the same week there were other such openings in Boston, Chicago, and Los Angeles; and a short time later, a Royal Premiere before the royal family in London, England. All the problems and conflicts that occurred during the filming were forgotten. Those who helped in the making of *Superman* enjoyed the applause for such a popular film.

With the huge success of the movie, *Superman*, both financially and popularly, Hollywood's battle of the comic books has begun. The year's highest grossing film in 1979, it made $150 million in box office income, not to mention the amount of Superman-related books, toys, and clothing that was also sold.

Fourteen movies based on published comics have gone into production already. Promoters and producers are actively looking for other comic characters to adapt to the movies.

Superman II, the sequel to the popular first film, will be released in 1981. In it, Villian Lex Luther and his two companions escape and make a surprise visit to Earth. They continue to seek revenge against Superman and Clark Kent. The same cast of characters will continue in their roles and the film promises to be as thrilling and action-packed as part one.

You may have already seen some of these movies:

Flash Gordon—a Dino DeLaurentis/Universal Studio release. Flash doesn't fly but some $25 million spent in making the movie makes him good competition for *Superman*. The Flash Gordon comic strip was used in the late 1930s. Buster Crabbe played the hero back then. In the modern version the hero is played by Sam J. Jones. Another relatively unknown face, Sam is being given a chance to become a star, just like Christopher Reeve was. The character Flash Gordon and his girlfriend, Dale Arden, fight their long-time enemy Ming the Merciless, Emperor of the Universe, in this movie version of the newspaper comic strip.

Popeye—from Paramount Pictures stars Chris Reeve's classmate from Juilliard, Robin Williams. Well-known for his leading role in the TV series "Mork and Mindy," Robin plays the part of the world's most famous sailorman. The budget for *Popeye* was some $13 million, and it is partly a musical production. Popeye and his girlfriend, Olive Oyl are just like in the original comic strip.

Conan the Barbarian—another Dino DeLaurentis/Universal Studios film. The writer and director is John Milius who wrote the screenplay for *Apocalypse Now*.

This comic strip film promises to be a more violent story than that of *Popeye* or *Superman*. The main character, Conan the Barbarian, is a sword-swinging hero who thinks that the best way to deal with his enemies is to kill them before they kill him.

Annie and Alley Oop—A project of Columbia Pictures. Comedian John Belushi is being considered for a leading role.

Terry and The Pirates, *Sheena, Queen of the Jungle*, and *Wicked Wanda*, all will be from AVCO Embassy Pictures.

Tom and Jerry is being released by MGM.

Tarzan—also a remake of an old-time film, is a project of the same company that made *Superman*, Warner Brothers.

There are also proposed versions of *Batman*, *The Silver Surfer*, and *The Daredevil*, which are not yet in the works.

Hollywood is turning to the comics for more reasons than just the success of *Superman* (although potential profits is probably a big one). Producers and directors believe that moviegoers are getting tired of space adventures and science fiction films. And they're turned off to serious dramas and heart-breaking post-Vietnam War stories. People in Hollywood feel that comics provide a source for stories that are well-known, fondly remembered and have a broad appeal to all kinds of people. Comic books, they say, are part of our American culture—almost like fairy tales.

Most of the comic book films will be entertainment that every member of the family can enjoy.

X
The Next Step in Chris' Career

"Well, it's Saturday today, and my cape's in the wash . . ."

One of Chris's main concerns after the completion of the movie was how to shed his Superman image. Some critics think that the role of "The Man of Steel" is limiting for Chris in his long-term career. For quite some time he was worried about being typecast in that mold. "The worst thing that could happen would be for me to become Superman forever," he said. "I plan to spend the rest of my life as a working actor, not as the actor who once played Superman."

Chris is making a serious effort not to turn into a product. So far he seems no different as a person than he was before he became the star of *Superman*. He has even consulted veteran actor Sean Connery, who suffered from being known only as James Bond. Connery advised Chris to do his absolute best the first time, but to try to avoid sequels, and to move into different type of roles as quickly as possible.

Even in public, Chris tries to remind people who he really is. "When people come up to me and ask, 'Are you Superman?', I'll say something like 'I was,' or 'No, I'm Clark Kent,' or 'Only from nine to five.' "

He feels that the public will come to understand all of the posters, toys and other merchandising efforts of Warner Brothers are selling a character, and not the actor himself. He says, "I think people will take you for who you say you are. I'll say, 'Hello, my name's Christopher Reeve and I'm delighted to play Superman.' "

He proved that this philosophy works for him. One time while filming was still going on, Chris attended a kid's birthday party. All of the guests had been told, in advance, that Superman was coming to the party. And Chris arrived wearing corduroys and a lumber jacket. All the children were asking for Superman over and over again, until Chris finally told them, "Well, it's Saturday today, and my cape's in the wash . . ." That was okay for both Chris and the kids.

Chris is pleased by most of the fan mail he receives. Some people write to him and say they can't wait to see him in another movie, like perhaps a comedy. Others tell him they would like to see him become another Cary Grant.

He finds a particularly heartwarming side to being identified as Superman through some of this mail. Some people, he feels, relate to Superman and look to him for strength. He gets letters from people in all walks of life; from mental health clinics and from some who are very ill. They view Superman as someone who gives them hope and can help them overcome their problems. Chris hopes that the belief in this superhero can do some good for these needy and sick people.

Chris learned a lot of both positive and negative things from other successful actors. These have helped to form his attitude toward his career.

He recalls having co-starred with Katharine Hepburn in the Broadway play, *A Matter of Gravity*. "What I learned from her was simplicity," he said. "She's a living example that stardom doesn't have to be synonymous with affectation and ego."

In spite of the fact that he has become what Hollywood calls a "superstar," Chris still leads a rather modest life. He drives the same battered 1970 Pinto he has had for many years. Chris still has his old "hole-in-the-wall" Manhattan studio apartment on West 83rd Street, although he has also added addresses in London and California—for convenience sake, he insists. He could care less about clothes. "I'd never make the Ten Best Dressed list. I've worn the same clothes since I was sixteen. I have one belt," he says with a chuckle.

Chris wants to be sure that he doesn't have the same trouble adjusting to fame that some other fast-rising young actors encountered. He says, "Sometimes, for certain people, the distance they have to travel emotionally from their beginnings to stardom is too much for them."

Freddie Prinze is one example of a young star who couldn't handle the distance from Harlem to Hollywood. After his death, people realized that his life as a star developed too quickly for him and he couldn't keep up with the fast pace.

"Sometimes it's harder to be famous than unknown," Chris says. And he remembers what happened to actor Warren Beatty, someone he knew fairly well. After his success in the movie *Bonnie and Clyde,* he just didn't feel like coming down out of the clouds.

Chris talks about the time he used to know John Travolta in New York before that actor became famous. But now he's too busy and too protected to even get together with some of his old-time buddies. "I can't believe that people who become phenomena like Cassidy, Travolta and Winkler find *that* is the reward they were looking for," observes Chris. "That's why they're running away, buying mobile houses and Learjets to disappear from it all." Chris insists that he will try to prevent his life from going in that direction. He considers himself reasonably talented, but certainly does not feel he is God's gift to the world.

What does Superman do for an encore? Well, Chris has had many options from which to choose.

"The three months after *Superman* opened, I didn't have space to breathe," Chris recalls. "I nearly drowned in telephone calls."

He doesn't want to divide his career into before-and-after *Superman*. Despite the fact that many people, especially his co-star Margot Kidder, said,

"He will be a major, major star someday," Chris refuses to move permanently to Hollywood. He explains, "I'm not a bad actor after all. I'm reasonably happy, reasonably sane, reasonably positive. Enough people seem to like me, I like enough people—so I'll settle for that."

Chris took his time in selecting the next step in his acting career. New offers poured in for all sorts of roles ranging from period dramas to satirical farces.

Some of the roles that were suggested included a factory worker in Georgia during the Depression, a college kid in Yale in 1890, and a piano player behind the lines in Germany before the war.

He rejected all scripts offered him for action-adventure stories that portrayed Superman-like characters. He turned down an invitation from Britain's National Theater because he wanted to give movies another try. He was offered film roles playing opposite such famous female leading stars as Goldie Hawn and Ali MacGraw. TV recruiters tried to get him for a CBS Special playing the dramatic role of Thomas Wolfe.

A really big part Chris said no to was the lead in *American Gigolo*, which was offered to him when John Travolta walked out on it. He defended that decision saying that the script was especially written for John, and Chris didn't think there was enough time before going into production to do a good job rewriting it to fit his own acting style. Chris's agents were mad though, because the offer had included a $1 million contract. He wasn't money-hungry. He just wanted to find the right next step to take in his career.

Aside from the leading role in a new movie which Chris finally decided to accept, he still had to finish shooting on *Superman II*. Although much of the filming on the sequel was done simultaneously with the first film, there was still a substantial amount of work to be completed on the picture. This would most likely be his last appearance as Superman.

Filming was supposed to begin in the summer of 1979, but production was delayed because of some difficulties with the script and the director. Richard Donner, who had directed the first film, had been fired. Chris was afraid that the sequel wouldn't be put together with as much care as its predecessor had been.

The producers had accidentally let Chris's contract for the sequel run out, and in order to get him back for the filming, they had to renogotiate with him. Money wasn't one of his greatest concerns he claims, "I agreed to the money in two days." What Chris did want, though, was some artistic control over how the movie was put together. Though the contract was signed, and the movie filmed, it remains to be seen whether Chris's concerns were taken into consideration.

XI
A New Movie

"It's my way to escape the cape."

Chris carefully chose a new picture called *Somewhere in Time*, for his first movie since *Superman*. As he put it, "It's my way to escape the cape."

The script is a gentle, romantic story based on the 1975 novel *Bid Time Return*, written by Richard Matheseon. And working on it was quite a contrast to the hugh production involved in *Superman*. This movie had a mere $4 million budget (as compared to the multimillion-dollar amount spent on *Superman*.)

When he was sent the script, nobody thought he would even consider accepting the role. Taking the part didn't exactly thrill Chris's agents, either. He had just turned down a $1 million contract for *American Gigolo*, and the producers of this film could afford to pay Chris only about half a million dollars. That seems like a big raise compared to the $250,000 he made for *Superman*, but his agent felt that such a well-known star should receive more money for his talent and his name. They advised him to wait for a more important role with a better-known director and big-name stars playing opposite him. They said, "You might not be so *hot* ever again."

But Chris is not easily swayed by the people around him. After all, he is a true Libran in personality. And once a Libran makes up his mind he wants to do something, he goes ahead and does it.

"My team to a man told me not to take the part," he says defiantly. "They said I should only do a movie directed by Michael Cimino opposite Jane Fonda or Barbra Streisand. But I like the story and I like the character . . ." So Chris signed the contract.

The level of interest for and belief in this movie was incredible—much more than for most Hollywood productions. Members of the movie crew worked for wages that were about 20 percent less than what they could have earned working on other movies. The director, Jeannot Szwarc and, of course, star Chris Reeve, could have commanded higher salaries elsewhere as well.

It seems to be the story that attracted such interested people to the project. Everyone, including the technical crew, was given a copy of the script to read before they were hired. "We wanted people who really wanted to work on this particular movie," the producer explained.

The director Mr. Szwarc, became well-known in movie circles when he stepped onto the scene just in time to save *Jaws II* from utter failure. Prior to that, most of his experience was as a television director.

The story of how he became involved in *Somewhere in Time* is a rather interesting one. Mr. Szwarc had been called to a producer's office to discuss a big-budget science fiction film. At the time he seemed like the right person for this type of film because of his experience on *Jaws II*. But Szwarc, not unlike other ambitious artistic people, wanted to try a different kind of movie—"an intimate love story like *Portrait of Jennie*." The producer, 32-year-old Stephen Deutsch suggested that Szwarc read *Bid Time Return*, whose screenplay had not yet been written.

The director was well aware of the possible problems that could be encountered in making a believable love story. He cited some examples of movies he considers failures—*Voices, Hanover Street*, and *Players*, and he tried hard to avoid repeating their mistakes.

He seems to have had a deep understanding of the story and how to portray its true feeling on the screen. He says, "The essence of romanticism is to show people and the world they should be idealized. We in [*Somewhere in Time*] have a strong and original obstacle between our lovers. They are separated by time."

The central theme of the story revolved around Chris who plays Richard Collier, a 1979 playwright. He has fallen in love with the photograph of a long-dead actress and journeys nearly seventy years backward in time to find and win her heart.

Chris was really interested in the character he portrayed—"A man who's incomplete. He had all the material things he needed, all the comfort, but he was missing a passionate commitment to something other than himself, and went in search of it."

The actor also accepted the part because he felt he could relate to the story. He was impressed because it wasn't slick or Hollywood cool as some movies are. And he really thought that he could make the audience believe he could time-travel. He said, "Hopefully, the audience will be absorbed with Richard Collier's motivations and stay with him."

The whole production was low-key. According to Chris's contract there would not be any popular song having the same name as the movie, and no merchandising efforts—some of the aspects of his *Superman* experience which he disliked so much. And no sequel was planned for this movie.

The author insisted that Chris Reeve was his and the producer's first choice for the role. They thought that his looks—big, handsome and strong —in combination with his acting ability—would enable him to approach the part with just the right sensitivity. "A cool, macho image would be ruinous to the movie," they said.

The director described Chris as "very cultured and amazingly proficient technically for someone so young."

And Chris had a lot of respect for the director who he fondly referred to as "boss." He jokingly pulled the director's bowler hat down over his eyes whenever he was on the set. A "preppie" as he still calls himself, Chris maintained casual friendships with all the people involved in the movie.

Most of the film was shot on Mackinac Island, Michigan, which is located between Lakes Michigan and Huron in northern Michigan.

The town is still very old-fashioned in many ways. No cars, trucks, buses or other forms of motor vehicles are allowed on the island. There is a ninety-two-year-old hotel, The Grand Hotel, in front of which much of the movie was filmed. There are real carriages drawn by hackneys and wagons drawn by horses still in use in the town. Bicycles are also one of the main means of transportation on the island.

The uniqueness of this town caused some unusual problems for Universal Studios which filmed the picture. They had to rent horse-drawn taxis, carriages and bicycles for the use of the cast and crew. Although generally against the town's rules, the movie crew was permitted to bring a twenty-seven-foot camera and soundtruck, a twenty-seven-foot utility truck and two forty-foot vans onto the island. But each time any of the vehicles traveled along the narrow streets of the island it had to be proceeded and followed by someone on a bicycle. And all the streets had to be cleared of horses first. Most of the props and camera equipment had to be transported on hay wagons. And since no trailers, which are traditionally used as film stars dressing rooms, could be brought onto the island, all three main stars had to take turns sharing the only available room inside the Grand Hotel.

When Chris first arrived on the island he was overwhelmed by the smell of lilacs which grow on bushes everywhere. But he soon found out about some other odors. As one crew member so effectively stated: "How intelligent to have so many lilacs in a town with so much horse manure."

There are some six hundred horses on the small island which is only about three miles long. This presented somewhat of a problem for the star. He is allergic to horses, and had to take a special decongestant pill every day. If he forgot, he was extremely uncomfortable and had to continually dry his watery eyes throughout the day. While all the other actors were driven to the set by horse-drawn taxis, he rode a bicycle up the town's steep hills. Chris didn't seem to mind it too much though. He says that it certainly was a better way to keep in shape than working out everyday in a hot and sweaty gym (like the one in which he trained for *Superman*.)

Chris became an additional tourist attraction in the town whose main industry has been identified as selling fudge to tourists. "Eat the fudge, then see Chris Reeve," the crew said kiddingly. Tourists crowded the streets in the filming area every day to watch the action. Having a movie made in any small town created a lot of excitement and interest for residents and visitors alike.

Chris wasn't the only well-known actor in this

movie. Actress Jane Seymour was cast as the turn-of-the-century actress with whom Richard Collier falls in love.

Ms. Seymour is known for her numerous TV appearances. She has played many different roles on NBC's "The Big Event" limited series stories including: (1977) "Seventh Avenue," (1978) "Love's Dark Ride," (1977) "Killer on Board," and (1978) "Four Feathers." She won high acclaim for her 1978 role of Genny Luckett in the "NBC Monday Night at the Movies" drama: "The Awakening Land: The Saga of an American Woman." The story was about an American pioneer woman's courage and her love for her family, her husband and the land. Her association with the ABC spectacular space series, "Battlestar Galactica" was short-lived. Ms. Seymour had a role in the pilot three-hour episode, but did not continue in the series due to a disagreement with the producers.

These, and many other acting opportunities Jane Seymour has had gave her much experience from which to develop her characterization of her part in this new movie.

Christopher Plummer also played a role in *Somewhere in Time*. He has experience acting in romantic stories, having starred in the movie *Hanover Street* in 1979, a love story set during the time of World War II. He also may be remembered as having played the thief and killer opposite Elliott Gould in the movie *Silent Partner*.

For a short period of time, Chris Reeve and the movie crew got a break from the smell of lilacs and horses and fudge. Some of the movie was also filmed in Chicago. The setting was the Chicago Public Library's Blackstone Branch. In May 1979, the streets outside of the building were lined with children anxious to see a famous star. These youngsters weren't just waiting for any actor though. To them, Chris Reeve was still Superman. To help shake the image, Chris would often go outside to talk to his waiting fans, and show off one of the costumes for his new movie. He would even bring youngsters, a few at a time, inside to watch the filming. With all of his efforts and new appearance, will Chris Reeve ever shake the Superman image?

XII
A New Play

"I am the glue that holds the actors together in the story."

The year 1980 brought new challenges and opportunities to the handsome, now popular, young actor. He has traveled both physically and careerwise back to Broadway.

Although it was his motion picture roles that made him most famous, Chris has much more experience acting in the live theater. To his credit he now has some eighty-five plays, but only three movies, yet the public best remembers his few movie roles.

Many motion picture professionals are probably horrified by the idea that Chris chooses to pursue live theater rather than more films. With all the Hollywood stuff going for him right now, why has he surprised everyone and decided to live in New York? Chris feels like he never left the Big Apple—it's where he went to school, and where he got his

start. Besides, he loves living there, and claims he
will never get rid of his beloved "hole in the wall"
apartment. It's full of programs from his first
plays, old letters from his drama teachers and all
kinds of memorabilia that Chris can't bear to part
with.

And already Chris has adapted to living in the
city. While playing on Broadway, Chris does as
many other New Yorkers do—he rides the A-train
on the subway to work.

His agents are mystified, too, because he turned
down a $1.5 million film offer to star on Broadway.
But Chris insists: "I've always wanted to stay con-
nected to the theater. Once you hit it big in films,
there's a temptation to take it easy, to get by on
your personality and bankability. There is a whole
category of leading men—Ryan O'Neal, Lee Ma-
jors—who don't care anything about the process of
acting. It's not that I think I'm so good, but I've
always wanted to be a real actor. I've had a lot of
training, and I want to use it."

For his re-entry to Broadway, Chris accepted a
role in a new play *The Fifth of July*, which opened
at the New Apollo Theater in New York on Octo-
ber 23, 1980. It was a difficult transition to make,
not only in location and medium of acting (film to
live theater) but also in type of role. *The New York
Times* summed up the situation in its headline
"From Superman to Vietnam Veteran for Christopher Reeve."

Lanford Wilson, a Pulitzer Prize-winning playwright wrote *The Fifth of July*, one of a trilogy of
plays about the Talley family. The work is both

funny and dramatic. Although the subject may seem to be depressing, it is really a funny and human story. It is about a group of friends who were classmates at Berkeley in the late 1960s and who reunite in 1977. The characters are representative of the 1960s era, and the story is a commentary about life in the '60s.

Chris Reeve played the difficult role of Kenny Talley, a veteran who has lost both of his legs, and much of his will to live. Some reviewers credit him with having the leading role, but Chris claims that he is the anchor in the play. "I am the glue that holds the actors together in the story," he says.

One of the things that attracted Chris to the play is that his role is a very unique and demanding one. He has to understand the psychology and thinking of this deeply emotional character before he can play Kenny. Chris also helps deliver the message of the play through his character portrayal. The theme of this play is similar to that of the long-time popular *Our Town*—making the most of your life. The following line spoken to Kenny at the end of the play sums up the idea: "The important thing is to find your vocation and work at it."

Chris's physical appearance has once again played an important role in his success. A city newspaper reviewer refers to this in his write-up of *The Fifth of July*. "Physically, however, he handles the part extremely well, especially when he must execute a terrifying fall backwards, and by the end he has made us believe in and care for his character."

Preparation for the role of Kenny involved a

great deal of practice to achieve the proper movements. Since Chris played a crippled veteran, he had to learn to walk with crutches. Chris spent several months visiting a veterans hospital and talking to veterans about their problems and handicaps. He says: "Acting is knowing what you're talking about." First he had to learn about certain kinds of people, then he could act like them.

Chris really wants audiences to see *The Fifth of July*. He thinks that it's a very worthwhile play. Even though some people who purchase tickets might be expecting him to portray a Superman-like character, Chris doesn't think they'll be disappointed when they see this moving and thought-provoking play.

In addition to preparing for the role in the play, Chris also has to gear-up for each performance. He says that there's a certain amount of nerves and excitement that build up before each performance. He found himself approaching curtain time with a definite eagerness to communicate with the audience and to share his feelings as the character of Kenny Talley. And after each performance, he couldn't seem to unwind. Sometimes, Chris admitted, he was awake until after 3 A.M. thinking about the audience and the way he acted that night. But he loved it that way—it made him feel good.

Also in 1980, Chris has made a noticeable number of appearances on TV talk shows, at schools talking to acting students and in newspaper and magazine interviews. Although he doesn't believe in stars promoting their own movies, he will do a reasonable number of public appearances because he believes they can help him as well as the movie. He thinks that such occasions help audiences to know a little more about an actor and his personal and professional development. In Chris's case, he wants people to identify him as a talented actor, and not simply as Superman.

Recently on the Tomorrow Show, Chris spoke extensively about *The Fifth of July*. On the Merv Griffin Show he told audiences of his hobby of flying airplanes. On the show he played an original composition on the piano which he called "Ode to Sailplane." He said that the piece was inspired by a recent Sunday afternoon, peaceful airplane flight over the desert in California.

An interviewer on Public Television showed Chris playing tennis—one of his other favorite pastimes. Chris spoke that night of his dislike for competitiveness, and of the challenges he sets for himself.

People who once knew Christopher Reeve only as Superman are being given the opportunity to better understand him and admire him as a multi-talented, multi-faceted, very interesting human being.

XIII
What About *Superman II?*

"This one's gonna be a winner, just like the first one."

Chris has gone to all this trouble to escape the Superman image and to establish himself in a variety of acting roles. And he has actually made quite a name for himself in live theater, in movies and on T.V. Bingo—in flies *Superman II*, and with it more association between Christopher Reeve and the great cape!

Something unusual has happened with the release of *Superman II*, though. Unlike other sequel films, the American movie audience will probably be the last to see it. Warner Bros. decided to adopt a so-called backward pattern of openings—one which takes the film from South Africa, France, Spain, and Brazil in late 1980, to England, Holland, Denmark, and Germany in early 1981. The movie is scheduled to open in the United States in June 1981.

Usually, Americans are the first to see a major motion picture. But now producers believe that overseas markets have gained in their importance to a film's success. Also, in the case of *Superman II,* the creators feel that excitement for the movie may be heightened in America by delaying its release. Stars like Christopher Reeve and Margot Kidder are helping create interest by their T.V. appearances, which are actually designed to promote their own acting careers.

Each city in which *Superman II* has opened so far has enjoyed record attendance. These satisfied foreign audiences are indicative of what the producers can expect in America. And this foreign success is in spite of the fact that the Superman comic has its roots in America.

Audiences are giving high praise to stars Christopher Reeve and Margot Kidder for their excellent performances. Unlike the first movie, handsome Reeve is present throughout the entire sequel. In the original film, Reeve began his role about halfway through the story, as grown up Clark Kent. He is still very much the star and title role in *Superman II*. But some other characters gain in importance in the sequel. The three characters from Krypton—Ursa (Sarah Douglas), Non (Jack O'Halloran), and General Zod (Terence Stamp) come back into action, Superman's mom (Susannah York) returns and has a more important role since Superman's dad (Marlon Brando) was written out of the script for financial reasons.

The new director took advantage of the audiences' familiarity with the story and characters of the original film. *Superman II* gets right into the action, and reviews only briefly the scenes from the first movie while displaying the opening credits of the new film.

Chris' role becomes a more romantic one. His tricky disguise as Clark Kent can't keep Superman's identity from Lois Lane forever. Once she catches on that Chris' mild-mannered Clark Kent and Superman are one and the same, their relationship changes. They fly off to his arctic fortress where Superman decides to give up his immortal powers in favor of becoming the more worldly Clark Kent. His intention is to stick with Lois Lane. But later on he feels that having super power is important both to him and to the future of the world. The film concludes as Superman overpowers the three supervillains and returns to the Fortress of Solitude.

Superman actually has three different identities in the new movie. As the hero, he continues to rescue the heroine, Lois Lane, from her accidental mishaps. As Clark Kent, he once again portrays the clumsy newspaper reporter who is well-liked but who can't seem to get things right the first time. The influence of his childhood also is evident in the sequel. He grew up outwardly as a normal youngster, but having certain unexplainable super powers. Chris interprets the relationship of the three identities in a very romantic way. "The story is ultimately about that kid, trying to get out through the two disguises. Superman is educated for everything he needs to know on earth . . . except how to love."

What's interesting is that, as in the original film, the story is left somewhat dangling, leaving the door open to a possible *Superman III*.

In the typical Hollywood style, word is out that this sequel to the sequel is already in the works. The big question is how many times will audiences be attracted to a film about the adventures of the same superhero? Many sequels fail for the simple reason that people get bored. But, on the other hand, the creators, producers and directors feel they have a winner in both Superman and Christopher Reeve, and they don't want to overlook any opportunity to make a successful picture.

What does the star say about all this? First he predicts about *Superman II:* "This one's gonna be a winner, just like the first one!" He thinks the new director has done a fine job putting it all together and that the film carries all the charm and goodness intended in the original comic strip.

As far as *Superman III* is concerned, Chris now has the script and is reading it very carefully. He says that the director is anxious to proceed with the project, but Chris wants to consider this one very carefully before making a commitment. He says he is willing to do the film only "if it's something more than a rip-off sequel." He also wants to evaluate the other offers which he may receive, and other possible steps in his fast moving career.

Chris should have no trouble continuing the Superman role. One thing he dreads though is the body building diet and those strenuous sessions pumping iron.

Critics who have seen the *Superman II* film are once again complimentary to the cast. *Variety* says "Reeve again scores better as the benignly cocky caped hero, than as the falsely awkward mild-mannered reporter." Actually playing Superman is probably more difficult for Chris and therefore he has to work harder at it.

In part the future of the Superman saga rests on the shoulders of the young star. Should Chris decide to "shake the cape" forever, they would have a tough time finding someone to fill his shoes. On the other hand, the talented young actor has to consider the future of his own career first, and do what will help him get where he wants to go.

XIV
A New Business

"It's the safest way to travel . . . Reeve Air gets you there!"

Chris learned to fly more than once in his life. Actually he became an airplane pilot before he got the part as the flying actor in *Superman*.

In addition to flying as a hobby and for the sheer enjoyment of it, the actor also has a business interest in planes. He owns an airplane charter company. His equipment consists of several Twin Engine Barons, small aircraft which are easy to fly and convenient to land. Chris has two pilots working for him. However, he also has a commercial pilot's license and sometimes flies the planes himself when he isn't busy acting.

Chris loves flying and has been doing it for years. He took lessons and worked his way up from little trainers to sophisticated airplanes. This year he will have accumulated some fourteen hundred hours flying. That's considered to be a good deal of experience for a pilot. He also holds a multi-engine instructor rating which qualifies him to fly commercial airplanes.

Chris is often amused at his customers' reactions when he shows up to fly the plane. Passengers almost go into shock when they realize who the pilot is. "What I really love is when they show up to take a flight to Detroit, or Poughkeepsie, or wherever they're going—and when I'm free, I fly the plane myself. When they come out to the airport and see that Superman is the pilot, I can't get them to buckle their seat belts," Chris says.

Regardless of whether Superman is on the plane or not, Chris insists, "It's the safest way to travel—Reeve Air gets you there!" And he says that he hasn't had any serious flying problems so far.

He can recall only one incident early in his flying career in which he came close to danger. When Chris was just a student pilot he was flying back from San Diego to Los Angeles in a small single-engine two-seater aircraft. He had a friend in the right-side passenger seat, comfortably reading a book. Chris was flying the plane, enjoying watching the beautiful Pacific Ocean sunset out the left window. All of a sudden his friend looked up from his book and said "What about the jet?" Chris, taken completely by surprise replied, "What jet?" Then he noticed outside the right window was a National Airlines 737 jet coming right toward them. Reacting quickly and using what he calls "the see and avoid method of not getting killed," Chris skillfully avoided an accident.

Small aircraft pilots must have quick reaction time and be sharp-sighted. Chris practices constantly to maintain his ability. Every thirty days he is checked out by an instructor in order to fulfill the requirements of his license. He must demonstrate his knowledge of emergency procedures. Chris doesn't mind having to pass these tests because he wants to assure his passengers the safest possible trip. "It's good for Reeve Air," he says.

Aside from the business investment he has in flying, Chris also considers it to be great fun. Now that he's living in New York, he parks his private plane in Teterboro, New Jersey, where it's handy for him to use whenever he has free time.

He also used a plane to move all of his personal belongings from Los Angeles back to New York. He says: "You can't imagine all the stuff you can load into a plane!" On this particular trip Chris was carrying full fuel and 950 pounds of luggage. He flew solo when he moved, and packed the plane with furniture, and books and all kinds of things. The flight took him only nine hours, with two rest and refueling stops—one in Texas and another in Ohio. That's considerably faster than the move would have taken driving a truck or van across country—and a lot less tiring too.

Another time Chris flew his plane for pleasure rather than business was last summer. He was appearing in the play *The Front Page* at the Williamstown Theater Festival in Massachusetts. He used his flying skill to transport his co-star Celeste Holm on a round trip to New York after the play.

Celeste Holm, a well-known experienced actress, felt honored to by flying under the care of such a handsome young actor. Forgetting for a moment that Chris really wasn't Superman, she said, "I really wanted to go on his arm."

Actually, one of the reasons Chris was anxious to perform at the summer theater was to gain experience playing different kinds of roles. He earned equity scale pay, which is quite low when compared to his movie salary, but accepted it willingly for another opportunity to shun his Superman image.

XV
Chris, the Regular Guy

"I love the air and the water. It's the land I have a problem with."

There's a rumor going around that Superman is a "junk food junkie." "Superman isn't—but *I* am," claims Chris. He's really hooked on Oreos, Mars bars and coffee milk shakes, he says. But he does know how important it is to eat enough healthy food, too. He had to stop feeding his "sweet tooth," though, while in training for the movie. Putting on thirty pounds in such a short time was difficult, and he had to eat steaks, not Oreos, to do that.

One of his favorite pastimes is playing the piano. Having taken years of music lessons, Chris plays very well. He prefers the compositions of Ravel and Debussy, but plays other types of music as well. Even during his busy *Superman* filming schedule, he found the time to practice at least ninety minutes a day.

Chris composes music as well. Recently he played one of his own pieces during a television talk show interview. He proved himself to be a sensitive musician who has a good understanding of music form and composition. Although in his introduction he claimed he wasn't a great pianist, Chris played the music with great feeling and control over the keyboard. Viewers who saw the show will agree that he is a man of many talents.

His interest in music surfaced again when Chris was invited to the Harris Gallery in New York. He was there, not to play the piano, but to introduce a budding pianist at a recital. In his introduction Chris repeated his appreciation for good music by saying, "I'm here to listen to people who play the piano well."

Not intending to detract in any way from the elegance of the occasion, Chris dressed very informally for what was considered to be a high-class event. He explained, however, that he still doesn't own a tie and doesn't like to dress up.

He's also an avid reader. When the day-to-day reality begins to close him in, he buries himself in a good book—usually the classics. Chris especially enjoys reading the works of his father, a famous poet and playwright. Often while in the theater, in-between performances, Chris and some of his fellow actors will sit around backstage and do poetry and play readings. Chris is very proud of his father's achievements.

Chris escapes from the pressures of his career by fleeing from land. "I love the air and the water," he says. "It's the land I have a problem with."

Perhaps the courage to do all of his own stuntwork and flying scenes in *Superman* came from his hobby of flying. He owns both a plane and a glider, and claims that flying them gives him a sense of freedom. "I defy you to be twelve-thousand feet above the Mojave Desert in a glider and worry about your job or your bank balance." The air allows you to stay up if you understand it," he insists.

Chris admits that his hobby might be slightly dangerous. He's had a few close calls with his glider despite all of his flying experience. And he is continually kidded about the time his glider was forced down into a top-secret defense area in Buckingham, England. That was the time when Chris's flying actually went out of control. Just after the filming of *Superman,* he was piloting a glider over the countryside in England. Hot air let the "Man of Steel" down when the thermals gave out. Chris was forced to coast to the ground and he landed in the middle of a secured research facility.

Here's an explanation of what might have happened to Chris on that fateful day. A thermal is an air mass which rises because it contains water vapor or warmer air than the air surrounding it. As it rises, the air mass increases in size by combining with the air around it. The air mass becomes like a large bubble which grows as it gains in height. While rising, the atmospheric pressure around it is reduced causing the air surrounding the bubble to cool down. The moisture in the thermal will then condense to form a cumulus cloud, releasing extra heat which helps the keep cloud afloat. The life of this cloud is of particular importance to a glider pilot. If the thermals do not keep recreating themselves, a glider such as Chris' cannot stay up. When the large cloud begins to lose its force, it will start to descend and evaporate. The cooling air of the air around it will cause strong currents, and these bring a glider down.

A pilot must therefore learn to recognize thermal clouds which are beginning to evaporate, and avoid flying near them. Luckily, in Chris' case no one was hurt. But you can be sure that this "super-pilot" has learned to recognize these potentially dangerous air masses, and will not fly his glider near them.

He also competes for more than just acting roles. Chris likes to travel around the world doing gliding competitions. He achieves great satisfaction from being successful at this difficult and challenging sport.

Gliding is air sport which is the counterpart of sailboating in the water. Some people may think that its too scary to be so high up in the air without the support of a motor. But glider pilots agree that riding on invisible atmospheric currents brings them a special kind of free feeling. They enjoy having nature in control during the time the energies of the sky help them stay afloat. Chris says that he feels so peaceful whispering quietly alongside a mountain ridge, or being carried upward by a rising thermal cloud.

The sport began as far back in time as the year 1178, when an unnamed adventurer leaped from a tower, using the billowing sleeves of his white robe as wings. Today, gliding enthusiasts use much more safe and sophisticated equipment. To be sure, Chris has studied the sport thoroughly and uses more than just his cape to keep him afloat.

Recently, however, flying has become more than just a sport for Chris, since he became the owner of Reeve Air.

Chris enjoys two other sports, both of which are on the ground though. For a person who at a young age was very clumsy and all legs, Chris is both a good skier and an avid ice skater. The way he darts around the ice, no one would ever believe he was uncoordinated. He does figure eights and circles on the ice with such a smooth, even motion that at times he looks as though he's flying.

In skiing he maintains excellent control, even on the toughest slopes and around the dangerous moguls.

Chris says that his height presented some problems for him when he originally was learning to ski, but now there's no stopping him. His private plane often comes in handy to fly him to some of the best ski areas in the country. Hidden behind goggles and a ski cap, the celebrity doesn't have too much difficulty concealing his identity from star-struck women and autograph hounds. Skiing is another sport which allows Chris to enjoy the outdoors and the beauty of nature.

When not in the air or on the stage, Chris spends much of his spare time on the water. He's also an avid sailor. On vacations and in between acting jobs, he does yacht deliveries for people. The last such excursion he made was for a man who lives in Toronto. The wealthy investment broker had been docking his well-equipped elegant boat in Connecticut, and he wanted it somewhere else. It seems as though he could only take time off to sail on a certain weekend, and he wanted to do it off the beautiful island of Bermuda. So he hired Chris to sail the yacht to Bermuda and have it waiting there for him when he got off the plane that special weekend.

This was a wonderful, relaxing way for Chris to spend a few days. He got together a crew of five other guys. They stocked the very comfortable boat with lots of beer, Ritz crackers, Sara Lee banana cake and their favorite "junk foods" and sailed it down to Bermuda. Upon its delivery, return airplane tickets were waiting for their trip home. "Six days and five nights . . . that's living to me," explains Chris.

He talks about why he considers the air and the water good escapes for him. "If you're out five-hundred miles off the coast of South Carolina and you see a force-10 gale coming, you know what you must do to survive it. Show business is devious, people maneuver, people play games. But in the sea or in the air, it's clean and it's direct and it's simple." Chris feels that his skill as a flier and as a sailor give him a great deal of control over his own fate. But the theater and the movies are a different situation. There the actor has to be dependent upon so many other people to achieve success.

Aside from these main hobbies, in what is left of his free time, Chris also enjoys playing tennis. This popular sport also requires good coordination and skill which Chris has demonstrated on the camera and the stage. One thing about tennis though which Chris isn't thrilled about is the competitiveness of the sport. "Competition doesn't come naturally to me," he says, and he really prefers the individual sports like skiing and skating. In these activities as well as the rest of his life, Chris sets obstacles for himself and then works to overcome them. He believes that progress in one's life comes from setting your own challenges and then doing the best you possibly can to succeed.

In spite of his quick rise to stardom, Christopher Reeve is a "regular guy." He tries to lead as normal a life as possible. He makes his home in a modest studio apartment, rides around New York City on a lime-green bicycle, does his own laundry, and buys his favorite snack foods at the local market.

He's also sensitive to other people. He remembers to send flowers and candy to his girlfriend, never forgets important birthdays, and is considerate of other people's feelings. Once he even sent Katharine Hepburn (the star in his Broadway debut show) flowers and champagne, just because he liked her.

Chris has received recognition for being the terrific person that he is. The U.S. Jaycees named the star one of the ten Outstanding Young Men for 1981. This prestigious award was given to him because he arranged special movie showings for orphans. The Jaycees felt that even though Chris was busy with his career, he still took the time to help make some children very happy.

Even during his college days at Cornell, Chris had earned a reputation for doing good things. His former dormitory advisor recalls that Chris was instrumental in establishing a special residence hall for students interested in acting. Chris saw that there were special houses for foreign-language students, and realized that acting students could also benefit from living together in the same residence and sharing their daily problems and experiences.

Actually, Chris is very philosophical about his relationship as an actor to young children. He says that there's a trap in having played the part of a character like Superman. Sometimes he feels like he has to be a moral guardian of young Americans. And although he avoids public appearances being associated with Superman, he enjoys entering the territory of kids under ten years old. "Believe me, I do 'The Muppet Show' and 'Midday Live' with Bill Boggs just to keep Superman and the kids in touch with one another. Now that, I think, is part of my responsibility," he said.

As far as his personal life goes, Chris tries to keep most of it a secret. He does admit that he has a steady girlfriend, though. Her name is Gae Exton, and they have been going together for several years. He claims they have no immediate plans for marriage, but they do spend lots of time together.

Chris laughs about the funny situation in which they first met. He was in London during the filming of *Superman*. He was waiting in line to have lunch in a cafeteria when he accidentally stepped on the toe of a woman behind him, who happened to be Gae. "I know it sounds like something out of a Cary Grant movie, but I swear it's true." He insists that Superman never lies.

What's even more interesting are the circumstances surrounding their meeting. "Despite the fact that I was still dressed as Superman, I made no first impression on her at all," Chris recalls. He justifies her reaction to him by explaining that being British, Gae didn't really know who Superman was, or that the American movie was being filmed in the neighborhood.

"She just thought I was a large American person with black hair and red boots. That was one of the things that attracted me to her—she was and is singularly impressed by celebrities . . . that quality is very attractive to me, because you know you have to sink or swim on your own personality," says Chris.

They have been going out every since then and Gae has accompanied Chris on many of his public appearances, as well as his off-camera outings. He calls her his "real Lois Lane."

Before he met Gae, and before gaining fame as Superman, Chris' life was rather quiet and unromantic. He used to travel the singles bars in New York and didn't have a very high batting average when it came to meeting women. "I used to get bad attacks of cold feet, and I found it difficult to approach a young woman sitting at a table alone," Chris confesses. He wasn't too creative, either when it came to reciting that "opening line" in which he would try to introduce himself. And he disliked the strange looks some women would give him. Now, most women would give anything to meet the superstar, but he's dedicated to Gae!

Playing the field didn't appeal to Chris. He's glad he now has found true love. "That phase of my life was entertaining, up to a point, but it's also embarrassing and hard to communicate with someone you really don't know," he says.

During the filming of the movie, there was talk of Chris dating co-star Margot Kidder. But both say there's no truth to the stories. "He's like my brother," says Margot. Though they did go together to the New York premiere of *Superman*, Chris insists they're just good friends.

Besides, nobody would ever believe it if they were dating—that would be too much like a fairy tale. Those kinds of fantasies never really happen. Chris and Margot lead such busy, private and professional lives that they hardly have time to see each other off the set.

Chris continues to lead a very private and low-key existence. He takes his work very seriously. He is, he admits "still at a stage where I'm taking care of myself, my career, first . . . These are the building years for me." He has worked very hard to achieve the success he has up till now, and he wants to stay on top.

He says, "The public has the right to look for spicy stories, if that's what it wants. And I have the right to say what I want to say, always." He doesn't want to avoid anything, but he simply "wants to be myself, and not somebody else's picture of me."

Vital Statistics

Name:	Christopher Reeve
Birthdate:	September 25, 1952
Place of Birth:	New York
Astrological Sign:	Libra
Height:	6'4"
Weight:	188 lbs. 214 lbs. as Superman
Eyes:	Blue
Hair:	Brown
Home:	Manhattan and Los Angeles
School:	Cornell University Juilliard School
Hobbies:	Flying, Sailing, Ice Skating, Skiing, Tennis
Musical Instrument:	Piano
Style of Dress:	Casual; The "Preppie" look
Favorite Foods:	Oreos, Mars bars, Coffee milk shakes, Sara Lee Buttercrumb Cake

CAREER CREDITS

Fifth of July.. Broadway
The Front Page..................Williamstown Playhouse
                                        Massachusetts
Superman II ....Warner Brothers
Somewhere in Time...................Universal Pictures
Superman ....Warner Brothers
Gray Lady Down .... Universal Pictures
A Matter of Gravity.............................. Broadway
Love of Life ....CBS-TV, New York
Irregular Verb of Love .... National Tour
Our Town .... McArthur Theater
Much Ado About Nothing   Washington, DC
The Games........................... Loeb Drama Center
A Month in the Country   Massachusetts
Death of a Salesman
The Hostage
Threepenny Opera
Troilus and Cressida...............Shakespeare Festival
                                        California
Private Lives ....Boothbay Playhouse
                                        Maine
Yeoman of the Guard ....McCarter Theater
                                        Princeton, NJ